I'M HER DAD

way back, mom, and I know you are already the best dad ever! I pray this book blesses you!

It's not all
Tea Parties and
Toe-Dancing. . .
AN HONEST GUIDE ON THE
ADVENTURE OF RAISING GIRLS

Brian Opbroek

HIGH BRIDGE BOOKS
HOUSTON

Dedicated to KaLyndia and The Girls,
owners of the 50 toes that matter to me most

Contents

Introduction: Sticky Boobs? What? _____ vii

1. Dad's Hats _____ 1
2. Dad, Security Detail _____ 15
3. Dad, Communications Director _____ 51
4. Dad, Her First Love _____ 77
5. Dad the Dean of Discipline _____ 107
6. Dad the Liberator _____ 141
7. Dad the Issues Manager _____ 171
8. Dad the Guru _____ 201
9. Dad of the Future _____ 217

Afterword _____ 241
Acknowledgments _____ 247
Bibliography and Works Consulted _____ 251
Index _____ 255

Introduction

Sticky Boobs? What?

What in the world are sticky boobs? And why am I the one asking this department store lady to help me find some?

Welcome to her world, Dad ... Brace yourself ... This could get crazy.

If you just became Dad to that precious bundle wrapped in pink, relax ... You have a lot more to worry about before you need to know what sticky boobs are. Indeed, it will be a while before you come to terms with all the hidden elements of the female world, but just so you are not completely blindsided, I wrote you a book.

Sugar and Spice

I am just a dad ... a dad with four grown daughters. They are phenomenal ladies, living some great grown-up lives, but they used to be little bitty girls just like yours. My greatest joy was being their dad (and their mom's husband), but now my greatest pride is to point in one of four directions and say, "I'm her dad."

You could say I just got lucky. Maybe life dealt me four fantastic hands in a row. I would have to agree because fortune certainly smiled on me with these little girls. After all, who would not want to be the honored guest at scores of sweet imaginary tea parties? What could be more valuable than the moments in the kitchen when they danced atop my toes to their own heart's music?

I am indeed the luckiest man alive for getting to be Dad to these four girls, but it was not all lady luck … and it was not all tea parties and toe-dancing.

For the record, girls are not 100% sugar and spice with everything nice. Raising them is seasoned with some bitter struggles and a whole lot of keeping your fingers crossed. Whatever ingredients your girl is made of, though, the woman she becomes has everything to do with who raises her. For your girl, that guy is you. She must have lucked out too, because you will be the best dad she could ever grow up with.

Yes, We Know What Causes This

I always knew I wanted to be a great dad. I also wanted to be a teacher, a pastor, filthy rich, and the president of the United States. Add to that my ardent desire to marry Charlie's Angel Jaclyn Smith, and there you have a summary of Brian Opbroek's childhood dreams.

As my destiny unfolded, I did become a teacher and a pastor, both rewarding careers in themselves. Riches, on the other hand, have eluded me, but there is still time for that. And to be president? Well, as my hair gets grayer, holding public office loses its appeal to me. As for the Charlie's Angel, I did marry a knock-out with an uncanny resemblance to Jaclyn Smith, so way to go, little dreamer Brian.

And now, four beautiful daughters call me their dad. KaLeigh, Bethany, Callie Ruth, and Sarah came to us one right after the other. We were that couple whom everyone felt obliged to ask, "Don't you know what causes this?" Our answer was simple, "Yes, we know what causes it, but we don't plan to stop doing it anytime soon." So in '95, '96, '97, and '99, we had some real fun proving the efficacy of that cause-effect relationship.

Those were busy years for us ... full of diapers, high-chairs, car seats, and—like I said—fun. What happened through the decades following those years birthed this book.

A Proven Theory

Raising our girls was like the testing of a great hypothesis. My wife and I believed we could prove the age-old claim that *love never fails*. We proposed that if we loved these girls deliberately from a solid definition of true love, then we would see four girls flourish in our home. So far, the theory has held true. Genuine love works so well that we might have proven a new theory: If whatever you are doing is failing, then it must *not* be love.

My wife is better at love than I am, but she insisted that I be the one to write this book. I guess "I'm Her Dad" would not sound right coming from her. Besides that, the Girls thought I should write it too, so here it is. I hope it makes them proud.

Early Planning

Back to my growing-up years ... From my early adolescence onward, I had determined to become a great dad one day. Having great parents myself gave me an early start in planning, but even great parents make little mistakes, so my first ideas for how to be a great dad came from keeping official records of all my parents' foibles. For this purpose, I began a journal entitled "PG–Parental Guidance Suggested." In this secret journal, I intended to make notes of how I would never do whatever my mom or dad might have just done, which I thought was not "fair." Haha.

Please remember, we are talking about a clueless, early adolescent boy who thought he might be the president one day. So it was with high hopes I wrote in this journal, where I would plan out my path to become the greatest father the world had ever known. If that meant I had to keep a ledger of my mom's and dad's deficiencies, so be it.

I remember, for instance, spilling a glass of milk one day, to which my dad reacted with a rebuking scowl and a gruff interjection of words which made me feel stupid. That day, I ran to my room and scrawled, "NEVER yell at your son for spilling a glass of milk!!!!!!!!" Little did I know I would never have a son, but if I did, I was darn sure not going to yell at him over spilled milk. (My dad, as I said, was the best dad ever, so do not believe a word from the journal of a boy who knew nothing of the price of milk.)

Sadly, when I was in my early 20's, my PG journal was ruined by a strange weather-related incident, so from that point on, I would be left to the perils of fatherhood without the epic wisdom of its pages. Yet I still wanted to be a great dad to these daughters my wife kept birthing. Lucky for me, a neighbor let me borrow a copy of a brand-new book—*She Calls Me Daddy* by Robert Wolgemuth. My neighbor was going on his second daughter at the time, while I was becoming the daddy of my third.

I devoured this great book before returning it to my neighbor. I never saw it again for the next 22 years, but it never stopped affecting me, and it effected many parenting skills in me for being Daddy to my girls. I thought about it so often through the years that when I sat down to write my own book, I feared my own experiences would sound as if they came from his pages, so I finally ordered a copy of the latest version for my home library. I checked it against *I'm Her Dad* and have done my academic best to textually credit *She Calls Me Daddy*, as well as Dr. Wolgemuth, for any specific lessons I gleaned from its pages. I hope any other similarities between our perspectives would be taken as an honor to him, for imitation is still the highest form of compliment.

Hope You Enjoy It ... And Hope It Helps

Finally, while the experiences recounted in this book are all in the context of raising girls, I trust the principles will prove gender-neutral for the most part. You dads of boys might not have to talk about sticky-boobs[1] as much as I did, but you still have to navigate some dangerous parenting paths. Sometimes you will not even be able to see the path, so you might feel like you are stepping blindly forward in hope.

Because I would like young parents' paths to be better illuminated, I have written this book. I hope it helps. Tuck the principles away in your heart. Not all of it will be for the moment you happen to be in now, but if pieces of it come to your mind at just the right time later, maybe I will have done my part to help someone be the dad he wants to be. I pray *I'm Her Dad* really does help you.

[1] Sticky boobs are a natural silicone adhesive bra your daughter will wear under a backless/strapless dress to provide seamless and invisible freedom with flexibility of movement. Now you don't have to google "Sticky Boobs."

1

Dad's Hats

"I'm her dad." If I said that once in the past 24 years, I have said it 10,000 times. According to conventional wisdom, 10,000 times is supposed to make an expert, so I guess it is time for me to write a book.

Just kidding. I am not an expert, but I have always liked saying, "I'm her dad." Whether one of my girls was receiving her All-American cheerleader accolades or being nominated for a student government office, I was proud to tell people, "I'm her dad." As I said, thousands of proud moments have presented themselves for me to say this over the years. In other instances, like when I might notice a young man prowling near her in the school gym, I say "I'm her dad" with a firm handshake. In those moments, "I'm her dad" means, "You might want to remember she's my daughter."

It really means a lot of things. It means I am the one who loves her more than you. I am the one who holds himself responsible for her best interest and sometimes for her actions. It means I am the one who teaches her to change a tire, or I am the one who holds her hair back when she is throwing up in the toilet. I am her dad. Sometimes I am her disciplinarian; sometimes I am her friend. Sometimes I am her spiritual leader; other times I seek her prayers. It means enough different things that I decided to share my "I'm her dad" experiences with you.

I could be wrong, but I am assuming you are someone's dad too. If that is you, I believe you will love this book. I also believe your daughter will love you for investing your time in a book like this, making an investment in being her dad. When your daughter thinks of her dad, she sees a whole world of different roles you play in her life. She adores you. She respects you. She trusts you. She needs you. Your daughter is a treasure entrusted to your care, and you are about to be the best dad she could ever dream of.

Of course, this book is not going to do all that for you; you are already doing that for yourself just by picking up tools like this book. Some of the principles in this book will stick with you for life. Some of them might become the very foundation of your relationship with your daughter. On the other hand, some of the approaches I take to things might show you exactly how you do not want to do things because it is just not you. However that works, thanks for reading my story.

I get to say, "I'm her dad" when I look at these four wonderful women who make me very proud. Who they are now owes a lot to the ramblings of this book, so let's look at what this book is ... and maybe what it is not.

What This Book Is and Isn't

This book is not psychology. I am not qualified for that. To be fair, I do have a few college hours in psychology but probably just enough to make me dangerous. As part of my teaching education, of course I learned a little bit of adolescent psychology, which naturally lent itself to my parenting paradigm, but I do not suppose I am qualified to give anyone real advice concerning the psychological development of their children.

Again, thank God that is not what this book is about. If any sort of psychological mumbo is mentioned in these pages, I'll be sure to footnote the source so you can know it came from a real psychologist, but I hope what you find as you continue reading is just advice plain and simple from a dad who made it through without altogether losing his mind. Not only did I not lose my mind, but I have to say I am proud of the ladies my little girls have become. I guess if that much were not true, you would not need to read this book. Who needs a book by someone whose ideas did not actually work?

With that said, however, you will find it embarrassingly clear that this book is also not a brag-session of parenting successes. Rather, you could probably call it a collection of converted failures in the exploratory project of parenting.

Converted Failure

Converted failure seems to be the mark of most of my life's undertakings. When I failed in one business venture, for instance, I had to "convert the failure" by changing my property's purpose. My dismal failure would now serve someone else's success, but at least I would cover my colossal overhead until I could get back on my feet. When I failed in business another time, I had to clean up an even bigger mess and "convert the failure" into just enough capital to pay Uncle Sam his share, to satisfy my debtors in full, and to keep my shirt. I might be relatively young, but I feel I have had enough failure to fill a lifetime.

I have failed so much that now I have grown weary of the rags-to-riches stories people write to lift our spirits from the muck and mire of personal disappointment. I should get an honorary history degree for all the anthologies I have read about the entrepreneurial American spirit's triumph in the face of failure. I used to find it encouraging that Edison never actually failed but rather found "1,000 ways the light bulb wouldn't work," but now his story is old to me, and I am trying to find out how to spend 10,000 hours doing just one thing so I can finally become a success![1]

Success through failure … I suppose you could say that phrase informed my parenting and gave me the content of this book. The look of helplessness in a daughter's eyes when her dad has flown off the handle might be the reason I consistently checked my anger at the door of our house. The cracking sound of a hesitant child's voice does wonders in teaching a man not to make his daughter feel as if she cannot express herself to him. The feel of a cold, unrequited hug will convince a father that tenderness might be more important than unbendable discipline. If success is defined by learning from failure quickly enough to make lasting change, then I guess you can say I had some successes with my girls.

The Apostle Paul once noted that he would rather brag about how God had helped him through his weaknesses than to boast of the obvious successes on his resumé. He even said that God's strength is made perfect through our weakness.[2] I do not advocate for excuse-making when it comes to weakness, but if someone else finds their answer through my weakness, then so be it. I suppose my weakness was worth it. I hope that is what this book becomes for young fathers doing their best to raise these precious daughters in their homes.

Learning from Others

So a lot of my parenting came from picking up the pieces of the collateral damage of my inabilities, but some of my better moments came by watching and listening to other parents.

As you read in the introduction, one of the avenues of development in my life as a dad was paved by the lessons in Robert Wolgemuth's book. I read the principles this great dad implemented in raising his daughters and tried to apply them to mine. Of course, I could never emulate his methods perfectly, and I'm not sure that would even be the goal of any pseudo-mentorship, but there were certain things I did as a dad, and even parts of this book you are reading, which would not have happened if I had not read *She Calls Me Daddy*.

In addition, I had great parents myself. Sometimes in the middle of a parenting moment, I would be able to look back over my shoulder into the farthest reaches of memory and pull out an instance when either my mom or dad had made a tough decision or expressed themselves in a way that made sense to my teenage heart. From their expertise, I was able to build my own parenting tool kit. Those memories also gave me insight into my own daughters' perspectives because there were plenty of times during my parents' great parenting when I as the kid did not understand they had my best interest in mind.

After my own parents' example of parenting come the many friends of mine who raised some great kids! I live in a community which to tell about makes out-of-towners often think I am lying. The people I have been privileged to do life with—my friends, leaders, colleagues, etc.—have all provided great examples for me to follow. I have truly lived a blessed life for having such good examples provided.

Bad Examples Are Still Great Examples

On the flip side of that coin, however, I have also had the privilege of observing some epic failures. I have served in the ministry for about 30 years, so you can imagine I have seen my share of people who have blown it. I have seen the dads who berated their sons their whole lives and then wondered why none of them wanted to take over the family business. I have seen the mothers who never learned to give their children freedom and wound up creating needy little adults who could not find their bearings, even if they had a compass, a clock, and telescope (the navigator's miracle trio). I have sat with parents whose hearts were torn out by the promiscuity or drug addiction of a teenager only to find out the parents were never present in their child's life until the problems began to embarrass the family. And now they are trying to find someone to blame.

That makes me think of the man who brought his troubled son to Jesus' disciples for healing. The disciples failed in the moment for reasons that would not be explained until later in the story, but as Jesus arrives on the scene, the dad seems to be blaming the disciples for not being able to help. "I brought my son to them," he says, "but they couldn't do anything."

It is funny how parents so often look for someone else to blame for not being able to help their kids once a problem fully manifests in their home. I love Jesus' answer to this dad just before performing a miracle for the boy. Well, actually, it was not an answer but a question, yet he was definitely giving this dad an answer with the question, "How long has this been going on?"

I love it. Jesus flat out says to the man, "Did you really just blame my disciples for something you have had happening in your home for years and years? Come on … I'm happy to help you, but you need to be honest about where this boy was when he started having issues. He was in your home! It might or might not be your fault, but it is certainly not my disciples' fault."

Many of us parents need to face this music. We also need to read the rest of the story[3] and believe that God can fix even the worst of our children's problems. However, even though God can mend any problem, do not let the lesson be lost: Dad, the problem happened under your watch!

As you can see, watching others has genuinely helped me, and if my observations of others can help a young dad or mom prevent some awful damage in their kids' lives, then so be it. I have seen my share of parenting blunders, but please know I would never point fingers except at myself. Even so, some of the parental warnings in this book are born from the wisdom of watching others. If you perused the introduction, then you also know my desire to be a great parent began when I thought I would keep a journal of all my own parents' mistakes.

That makes me laugh now—and I thank God that journal was accidentally destroyed—but the point remains that to learn from other's mistakes is wisdom. For you, maybe I can be the "other guy" who made enough mistakes for you to learn a little. That would classify you as brilliant. The truth is no matter whose mistakes you learn from, your kids will be glad you did.

Our Kids Are People with People Problems

The kids are the ones with the real challenges growing up in this world of ours, and every kid's challenges are different. Sometimes as parents, we forget that our kids want nothing more than for us to be proud. We get caught in strange and vicious cycles where both the parent and child forget the other one really would like the best for each other. It boils down, sometimes, to giving each other the benefit of the doubt and believing the best about each other.

Depending on where you are in your parenting journey, as well as how cynical you are, it might surprise you to hear one study's discovery that American teens "place high value on honesty and hard work, and the vast majority are thinking and planning seriously for the future."[4] In other words, our children and teenagers are not just bad little humans needing to be disciplined. They are people with dreams, desires, needs, and goals. Furthermore, if we as dads (and moms) step into the grown-up role we are supposed to be playing, we could offer our kids the encouragement and tools they need to work toward those futures.

The obstacles your kids face can seem insurmountable. Whether it is the social pressure to fit a certain mold or the quiet struggle of insecurity, rest assured your kids will have challenges.

My girls had the unique challenge of growing up as PKs. You might not be familiar with the term, but that's how Preacher's Kids often refer to themselves or, more often, get referred to. Preacher's Kids have the odds of public opinion stacked against them. They fall into a confusing dichotomy of stereotyping. One researcher pointed out that PKs often feel like they live in a glass house, where everyone feels free to watch and judge, expecting their clergyman's children "to either be rebellious hellions" or "perfect role models."[5]

If you think about this, Preachers' Kids are damned either way. They will either become self-fulfilling prophecies of people's hellish expectations, or they begin at a young age to carry adult-like role-modeling burdens. In the first case, the preacher's kid sneaks around performing the acts everyone has already assumed she is involved in. In the second case, she becomes a twelve-year-old adult counselor, proffering uncanny wisdom to church ladies who do not know who else to share the secret struggles of their marriages with. Either way, the preacher's kid can start life feeling under the gun.

My point is not for everyone to feel sorry for preacher's kids, and I am not expressing a "woe is me" moment on behalf of my kids. My point is simply that every kid has his or her own problems to deal with. When it comes to my girls, I am glad they were able to succeed even in situations where people typically expected to play audience to failure.

Your kids might not be PKs, but they have their own hard challenges to beat. I am sure every profession's progeny has to deal with issues that make them unique. Part of the point of this book is that parents who make themselves aware of the issues their own kids might face will have a much better chance of helping their kids through the issue!

Dads like you and me can be proactive in detecting potential challenges and equipping our kids to beat them.

Tools, Strategies, Tactics ... Hats ... Whatever It Takes

So dads like you and me need to be ready. We need the right tools in our toolbelt for all the situations we will face trying to raise these girls in our homes. I like the toolbelt analogy because it really flows with the "project management" picture *She Calls Me Daddy* painted for me so many years ago, but that's as far as I should steal the analogy for this book. Maybe, instead, let's imagine I am offering you "strategies and tactics" to maneuver through the "battlefield" of parenting your girls. Then again, that kind of warlike language might be overkill for our task.

Maybe we could just talk about all the different hats you and I have to wear as girl dads. That would work. I can think of several hats I had to wear, sometimes simultaneously. I had to be *Dad, Security Detail*; *Dad, Communications Director*; *Dad the Dean of Discipline*; and even *Dad the Guru*. Not all of these hats fit me perfectly, but you do what you have to do when you are handed a job that needs to get done.

One of the hats which fit me more naturally was *Dad, her First Love*. That might be because it's the natural hat every dad wears or maybe because I was born a romantic. That is a hat I will always wear. Two hats dads wear which might not come so naturally but are so important for our daughters if they are going to conquer this world and win their own destinies are *Dad the Liberator* and *Dad the Issues Manager*, letting her go and following her lead ... giving her a heads-up for the realities of the world. These Dad jobs take some proactive preparation.

That is what this book is for. Use it however you want. Read it straight through or jump around to the headings that pique your interest. Please just use it. It will not hurt my feelings if you disagree with some of it, but if something in it serves you, that is why I wrote it.

She Deserves It

All I am saying is that your girl deserves the best shot she can get. You are the man she has held in her highest esteem from the moment she first imprinted on you. She deserves to know her boundaries, and she deserves to know you will do your dead level best to protect those boundaries. She needs your strong disciplining hand as well as your soft, pain-discerning heart. She needs someone who can laugh at himself as he shuffles down the tampon aisle at Walmart but would never ever laugh at his daughter's expense. She needs somewhere to be vulnerable and somewhere to test her strengths. I did my best to toe the line for my girls, and I am offering our story on the chance that it might encourage you.

Be encouraged, therefore, just to be a dad to your daughter. You might indeed have other callings. Your life's mission statement might be three pages long. On top of that, if you are like me, you carry burdens that at times seem they could break you, but when this life is said and done—hear me … because I have been with hundreds of families laying their loved ones to rest—when it's all said and done, how you did the dad thing is what they're going to remember. How you did the dad thing is what will help them rest at night after you have gone to rest in peace.

By the end of this book, I will share with you some of the ways I found to keep myself healthy and grounded on a spiritual level. That chapter might or might not be your "thing," but please discover whatever your thing is because your daughter deserves it. It is, after all, kinda your fault that she is on this planet, so the onus falls to you to guide her, protect her, and show her how things work. That responsibility starts the moment she is born and ends … well, I have not figured out exactly when it ends. Since I do not know where it ends, we will end our journey wearing the hat *Dad of the Future* (Chapter 9).

As *Dad of the Future*, I hope I still have thousands more "I'm Her Dad" moments, but when this all started, I was just trying not to drop her.

Keeping her safe is scary. For that, you will need your first hat of *Dad, Security Detail*.

[1] Gladwell, Malcolm. *Outliers: Why Some People Succeed and Some Don't.* Little Brown & Co., 2008.

[2] 2 Corinthians 12: 9-10

[3] The Gospel of Mark, Chapter 9: 14-29

[4] Bostrom, Meg. Framework Institute, 2001, pp. 1–38, The 21st Century Teen: Public Perception and Teen Reality.

[5] Allman, Tara J. "An Analysis of the Stereotypes of Preacher's Kids and its Application on their Spouses" (2007). *Theses, Dissertations and Capstones*. 13. https://mds.marshall.edu/etd/13

2

Dad, Security Detail

So you placed covers on every outlet, doorknob, and sharp edge in the house. You installed a gate over the stairwell and the kitchen entry. You attached so many child-safety latches that the adults in the house will have to relearn how to open cabinet doors. You strapped your dishwasher and oven door; you wrapped your appliance cords; you removed every possible choking hazard; you threw away all your knives, medicines, and cleaning products; and you put a combination lock on the toilet seat with no thought for how sleepy you would be trying to pee in the middle of the night.

Good job. Now you have proven the value of your new housemate. It is obvious to everyone how much more this little life means to you than any of your normal conveniences (If you have not done any of these things—at least the sensible ones—maybe you could use a book like *Baby Proofing Basics: How to Keep Your Child Safe* by Vicki Lansky or some similar instruction manual on minimizing household child-related hazards).

Assuming you jumped straight into proactive baby-proofing as soon as you found out you were slated for fatherhood, we can move on to the challenges of the next 18 years or so. During your daughter's life in your home, she has a justified internal expectation that you are her protector. When she is a teenager and you play this role, she might act like a drowning victim and flail violently against your life-saving measures, but never forget, in her heart of hearts, she sees you as her border controller, her rescuer, and her superhero. She knows you are *Dad, Security Detail*.

I am not trying to romanticize this concept. I simply want to wake your father heart up to realize where your daughter's heart is. The role of protector is not something she consciously assigns to you; it is just natural. Call it evolutionary or call it Creative design. Call it whatever you want, but there is a natural obligation between parent and offspring for the parent to keep the offspring safe even at the risk of perishing.

Such a concept seems like a no-brainer if we are talking about a dad's willingness to run into a burning building to save his daughter, but apply this concept to her emotional well-being and the development of her life's boundaries and dads begin to cower. Whether it is the fear of the unknown, the fear of failure, or the fear of rejection, something stops dads from realizing their potential as the ranking officer in their daughter's security detail.

Do we give more thought to insuring our assets and ensuring our retirement than we do to protecting these most precious deposits of human potential entrusted to our homes? Well, maybe some men do, but you bought this book, so apparently, you do not. Apparently, your daughter is one of your most valuable investments. You must have discovered that she is a hidden treasure or a pearl of great price, worthy for you to sell all you have in order to keep her safe.[1] And since that is true, let's now turn to the many ways our daughters need us to establish their security and provide protection.

Identify the Threats

Just as you did when you childproofed your home, now it is time to evaluate the threats your daughter will face over the next few years. A few Christmases ago, I bought my youngest daughter a wilderness survival guide.[2] I wish I had bought one for each of my girls when they were younger. A survival guide is a perfect glovebox companion, right along with the seat-belt cutter/glass breaker that should be in her console. A survival guide catalogs threats and offers specific strategies for overcoming them.

As *Dad, Security Detail*, here is our broad index of threats: physical danger, emergency situations, personal ignorance, boys (and girls), predators, and emotional trauma. With each threat in the following pages, I am offering some strategies and tactics to overcome them. No survival guide can predict every problem exactly how it will play out, so you will want to adapt these ideas for your own home and specific situations.

Physical Danger

A dad is not a dad if he would not catch a bullet for his daughter. Protecting your daughter from physical danger is the most instinctual strand of your parenting DNA. The moments my daughters were in physical trouble will never escape my psyche.

One blistering summer day at our home in Louisiana, when my third daughter was only three years old, I was working on a DIY project on the backside of our property. I kept hearing—and ignoring—the faint sound of a car horn until something in this dad's heart said I could not ignore it any longer. I climbed down from my project and went to find out if it could be our horn. As I approached our driveway, you can imagine the fear that struck me as I saw my daughter's face swollen and red, as red as her beautiful hair. The details of how she got herself locked into the car and how she had the presence of mind to honk the horn are left to history, but the thought that she would not have lasted much longer if I had continued to ignore the horn has created an indelible fold in my mind.

Another time during another blazing summer a few years later, I looked down the side of a pool where we were gathered for a birthday party. My mind barely understood what I was seeing as this redhead once again was struggling for her life. From two feet under the water, she was looking up at me and making the motions of a useless dog paddle. The panic in her eyes said she had realized I might not ever look down to notice her. Thank God I did. No one else even noticed, but that day, I once again experienced the greatest fear and relief within milliseconds of each other as I was able to reach in and jerk her to safety.

I do not suppose any of that has to do with acquirable parenting skills to be delineated in a book, but they do demonstrate the fundamental drive in a dad to physically protect his daughters. I guess I could write, "Hey, Dad, you need to eat right, stay physically fit, and keep your reflexes sharp so you can save your daughter from all her distresses," but that is an unrealistic waste of words. If you are present and your daughter is in danger, you would not have to be told to save her life. You do not even need to be told that her first car's Consumer Report safety rating should outweigh its cool factor. You already know how to keep her safe in these situations.

However, we won't always be the ones making decisions for our daughter's safety, and even the best dads cannot always be present to protect their daughters from physical danger, so the next most necessary thing is that we prepare them to protect themselves. To do that takes purposefulness and proactivity. To leave it undone smacks of irresponsibility or maybe an unwillingness to entrust her safety to herself. But at some point, a girl's dad must realize she is going to be by herself in some situations, where his voice might be the only sensible one in her head. That is when you find yourself glad you wore the hat *Dad, Security Detail*. The one in charge of security will have taken time to prepare his girl for emergency situations, especially when he is not around.

Emergency Situations

One thing every girl needs from her dad is a heads up on how to deal with emergency situations, particularly those that present a threat to her physical person. For this chapter to be the first real "advice" in the book and considering that I just called out neglect as "irresponsible," I must say I did not do a great job in this area.

I never put my girls in CPR classes even though they were active babysitters. I never did the Brady Bunch dad thing, running periodic fire drills in my home, either. I never even took my girls to the gun safety class right down the road from our house—and we live in Louisiana, where people keep guns in every drawer.

However, we did at least talk about the best fire-escape route from each room in the house, and I reminded our girls *ad nauseam* that their first goal in any unfamiliar place must be to identify the exits and plan their escape. Additionally, when their school had lock-down drills, we reviewed the reasons for the school's rules. It is sad that active shooters have become a genuine threat to our schools, but these threats and so many others need to be deliberately prepared for, at the very least, through an awareness of the best possible reactions.

Weather-related emergencies, too, present horrific threats to our area of the country several times a year. Our girls have had to learn when to take the local warnings seriously and what items on the emergency checklist are the most important to complete as they hunker down.

Your daughter will soak up your advice if you talk to her as if you really believe she is worthy and capable of playing an integral role in life-and-death situations. Try it. You will see her perk up if you talk as though you trust her to do the right thing in bad moments.

If you do not have these talks with her, she might assume she is somehow mystically protected from harm or that it is other people's responsibility to know what to do in emergencies. She might play the role of the damsel in distress even if there is no prince charming riding to her rescue. Your deliberate attention to her personal responsibilities in emergencies will shake these notions and put her on the horse as a rescuer.

Keeping a cool head and taking a lead role in emergencies are difficult concepts to teach. For one thing, there is no way to know your girl has learned the lessons until you actually observe her go through an emergency … until you hear her make a 911 call with clarity and presence of mind. And *who* wants *that* to happen?

This element we are discussing now is like an insurance policy where you faithfully pay the premium but pray you never have to cash out the benefits. You would never let your insurance lapse, but would you leave your daughter unprepared for emergencies? Speaking of insurance, does she know how to call roadside assistance from the number on the back of her insurance card? Does she know how to change a flat tire when roadside assistance is not available? Does she know how to drool after an avalanche to let gravity tell her which way is up? (Neither did you, did you?).

Well, she needs to know these things!

The sheer fact that you cannot be present to save her every moment of her life should drive you to have these emergency talks. Only ignorance should stop you from teaching your daughter emergency skills, and ignorance can be alleviated with simple Google searches. Do your searches and teach your girl!

Personal Ignorance

Speaking of ignorance, that brings up the next thing dads must protect their girls from. Awareness saves lives. Naivety is your daughter's enemy. If all we do is allude to the dangers of the world and demand that our girls stay within our walls, be sure of this: our daughters will be drawn by the mysteries of the unknown. In other words, if we try to protect our daughters by promoting ignorance, their own curiosities will deliver them into the hands of danger.

You must tell your daughter plainly and honestly what the real dangers of this world are. Of course, making her walk in fear is not the goal, especially exaggerated fear based on your vague descriptions of the evils lurking outside your home. Instead, specific instructions about real-world issues will free your daughter to enjoy her world while never dropping her guard.

When I mention protecting girls from their own ignorance, the first image that might come to mind is the predator down the street who would take advantage of her in a moment of vulnerability. However, we have reserved predators a section of their own a little farther down in this chapter. For now, the list of safety concerns our daughters must be aware of is endless. It includes predators, of course, but what about life jackets, seat belts, barbed wire, wildlife, and mechanical malfunctions of things that were designed to be fun? What about the powers of water, fire, earth, and weather? The list could provide a topic-of-the-day for every day your girl lives under your roof.

You might not want to have family devotions every night concerning the dangerous world in which we live, but at the very least, seize little opportunities to vanquish ignorance from your daughter's weaknesses. Think of the many dangers your daughter faces which simple awareness could avert for her and her friends (who are most likely not being relieved of ignorance at home). Imagine the pride you'll feel when your daughter survives a traumatic event and says, "My daddy taught me to stay alert," or "My dad taught me how to use a fire extinguisher when I was eight years old."

Maybe a daily list of topics is not such a bad idea. If you make a list, send it to me. I will credit you if we include it in the next edition of this book.

Boys in General

At the top of most girl dad's lists is *boys* and their boyish intentions. It sounds like I am being facetious, but boys really do present a danger we girl dads have to think about.

When my first daughter was born, a friend of mine pulled me aside. Cover your ears or skip the rest of this paragraph if you do not want to hear what he said because he is one of those friends who knows how to put into words what everyone else wishes they could say. Anyway, he pulled me aside and gave me a secret: "If you had a son, you would only have one _____ to worry about … but when you have a daughter, suddenly you have to worry about a thousand _____s." I know that sounds crass (if you filled the blanks in correctly), but it was just crass enough never to leave my memory. Indeed, I had a lot to worry about when it came to my new daughter and the minds of nasty boys.

Since I am writing this in the 21st century, I must add that boys are not the only ones with eyes for your daughter anymore. The girls in her world might also be inclined to seek her attentions in a more-than-friendly way. I am not trying to be funny or prudish. Rather, I am just being honest about the raging hormones and rampant experimentation that pervades our society and from which dads can guard their daughters in healthy and empowering ways.

There is only so much a dad can do to protect his daughter from the thoughts of other adolescents. I remember the first time someone reported to me that a jock in a locker room claimed he would be the first to "tap" my daughter. I wanted to remove his tapper for him and bury it somewhere he would never be able to touch it again. But there was nothing I could do about that. What I could do was empower my daughters to ignore idiots and seek only the kind of boy who would be worthy of their attentions.

Part of the strategy for protecting our girls from boys has been saved for a later chapter. That chapter presents the secret weapon of treating your daughter better than any boy ever could so her standards move too high to be reached by underachievers.

Nevertheless, there are things we can talk about now to prepare ourselves for when boys enter the picture. First, know that you cannot ignore them. Ignoring boys will only encourage them. Instead, find lots of ways to talk about them. Mention them by name. Let it be known you have noticed them circling like vultures. Ask what your daughter thinks about them and dig deep to say things you know she hopes you are ignorant of.

I remember being an adolescent. I remember what it felt like to have a crush. I remember my heart beating faster and my breath shortening when a romantic scene came on the TV when I was a kid. I remember hoping my parents did not notice. My girls always knew the things I remembered about being their age. I believe that helped me protect them, indirectly. I also believe it helped them trust me.

Because KaLyndia and I had built trusting relationships with our girls, they listened to our opinions when we decided upon age limits and specific guidelines for dating, kissing, and having boyfriends. Those age limits and guidelines are important for you to discuss openly with your girl, maybe even helping her negotiate her own thoughts into the plans.

Maybe you can use your business skills for negotiating the matter. Maybe you can come to the table with tight terms and conditions but settle on what seems like a win-win to your daughter. I don't know what level of propriety and decorum you want for your household, but when you come to the table to discuss it, you must approach the subject with specific thoughts. You must show that you have thought your position through with reason. Then, even if your girl does not tell you, she will feel special and valuable because you have built protections into her life.

Even though she hems and haws about your views on the nasty boys in her world, she is hoping you will stand up and be the "bad guy" who tells her what the rules are. It takes skill and prayer to play the role of the bad guy, especially against boys who should not even be in your daughter's life. Your every move has to be interpreted (by her) as genuinely in her best interest. A wrong move can push a daughter into the arms of a nincompoop. However, if your daughter trusts that you are for her and not against her, she could even begin to trust your judgment better than her own.

My second daughter, who happened to walk into my office while I was having the computer read the previous paragraph back to me, suddenly blurted out, "Like me!" After I finished laughing, she reminded me of two exact scenarios where she not only trusted my judgment but needed me to be bluntly honest.

One was when she was nearly engaged to a young man who was not a perfect match for her. The other time was when she found the one who was perfect for her, but she kept getting cold feet. On both occasions, she wanted more than my opinion. She point-blank asked me to tell her what to do. In both cases, she needed me to be the strong arm of conscience because she felt her own might be too blurry.

For the record, my style is *never* to tell others what to do, but in these instances, she needed me to be the "bad guy" (or the "good guy" depending upon how you look at it).

An old missionary friend, Irvin Rutherford, proved this same principle in his relationship with his two daughters. This sounds like a story from a different time and culture, but this dad literally picked his daughters' husbands out for them. When he first told me about this, I thought he must be some kind of old-school chauvinist who ruled his home with an iron fist. But I also met his grown daughters, who were happily married to men they considered perfect picks! Somehow this dad had earned the ultimate trust from his girls.

I don't think my daughters are going to take their trust of my opinion that far, but my point is as simple as this: the way to protect our girls from "boys" is to build enough rapport with them that they trust our boundaries and guidelines when we set them. If you can secretly get your daughter to see the boundaries as genuine protection, she will be happy to feel safe.

Physical Predators

As much as we need to protect our girls from nasty boys in general, a worse threat to their safety must be acknowledged and discussed in our families. The fact that the United States of America, as of February 2019, reports a total number of 550,394 registered sex offenders[3] tells us that we have a lot to talk about in our homes. This number represents "registered" sex offenders, which means people who have already been caught and convicted for a sexual

violation. Whether we want to face it or not, our neighbor-
hoods are full of predators.

The Liam Neeson movie *Taken* (2008) was released as
my oldest daughter was entering her teens. I admit, like
many westerners, this movie was one of my first eye-open-
ers to the problem of sex trafficking in our current world.
As you can imagine, a father of four young girls would be
riveted by a movie like *Taken*. Even the thought of my
daughters becoming the objects of a predator's sexual
schemes makes me willing to abandon my own morals and
resort to unbridled violence, but there is a huge difference
between me and former CIA operative Bryan Wells: I do *not*
have "a very particular set of skills that make me a nightmare to" sex traffickers. Even with my daughter's life on
the line, I would never be able to fight hundreds of armed
killers one right after the other and come out alive.

No, I would not be able to travel to the other side of the
world, break up a deeply entrenched sex-trafficking ring,
and isolate the sole transaction that would reveal my
daughter's whereabouts, all within 96 hours and under an
onslaught of bullets. However, I was determined to equip
my daughters with an awareness of the evils in this world
and within men's hearts.

For one thing, when each of my girls became old
enough to grasp the content, I made them watch this movie.
Beyond that, we have had countless talks and run-throughs
on how to remain alert in every situation. Dads must discuss with their daughters the dark side of this world and
how important it is to avoid it.

My wife and I established very solid ground rules for
our girls, like never accepting a ride with anyone they don't
know personally, never taking a sip from an open drink at

a social gathering, and never allowing their fate to be decided by irresponsible friends. These ground rules gave our girls confidence and boldness. They also opened the door to more freedom for fun because they had the assurance that comes with responsible forethought.

I would love to say my girls were all black belts in some style of self-defense, but even though my older brother is a Kung Fu Sifu, we neglected to enroll our daughters in his classes. Nevertheless, we did practice simple techniques of escaping someone else's grasp and seeking the quickest disengagement possible. We discussed the power of their voices and the idea that everything in their environment is a potential defense weapon. We even went so far as to ask our girls for a resolution of their will that they would die trying to escape the first seconds of an abduction rather than succumb to the untold horrors of compliance.

We could not let the uncomfortable nature of these fears hinder the conversations that could give our girls a fighting chance. We determined that a healthy fear of the evils in this world might keep them safer than just hoping nothing bad ever happens.

I do not necessarily advocate for young ladies to train in concealed weapons management because, with much less liability, training with a bottle of pepper spray can serve the same purpose of reducing immediate threats to their person. Regardless of what you choose, however, self-protection must be a routine part of your fatherly input.

When my 24-year-old planned a trip to Europe with a friend, I insisted that she call the sheriff's office to sign up for a weekend of awareness and defense training, which she did. My daughters are not expert fighters; that has never been our goal. I simply hope they know enough to help themselves identify predators, avoid traps as much as possible, and debilitate an assailant long enough to disengage.

With all this talk of training, however, we would never want to instill a false sense of strength or invincibility in our daughters. Sadly, no amount of skill can protect our kids from all harm.

One of the most shocking criminal incidents of our local area involved the 12-year-old son of a lady I had gone to high school with. As a great mom who wanted her son to be able to defend himself, Amy had her son Justin in regular Karate classes, but Karate or no Karate, his physical strength was still that of a 12-year-old. As evidenced at the scene of his final struggle, Justin did fight with all his might, but in the end, the strength of a grown man bent on evil overpowered the well-trained skills of the innocent child. Stories like Justin's are the reality of our world today, and we have an obligation to alert our daughters to the presence and intentions of predators.

Electronic Predators

I would never retell Justin Bloxom's story for shock value. The details of his story have brought about new laws in our state and, when told appropriately, have saved lives. One of the details explains how Justin's assailant lured him outdoors using an electronic device to pass himself off as a girl Justin would have known from school.

Justin was at a friend's sleepover when "Amber" texted him to say she thought he was cute and would like to hang out. She added that she did not live far away and could get a cab to the house where the sleepover was if Justin wanted to see her. By the time the cab came, the other boys had gone to sleep, so Justin went outside by himself to meet who he thought was Amber. It was not.

You might have seen the incident featured in a 2010 hour-long episode of "Web of Lies." That episode points out the shocking reality all dads need to hear: "It's easy to ignore or forget the millions of people who suddenly have access to your life online, but behind the clever screen names and witty captions hides a dark digital world with real dangers and risks."[4]

In *She Calls Me Daddy*, Robert Wolgemuth put it better than I ever could. Warning us about our daughters' electronic devices, he writes, "… she's literally holding in her hand a portal of incoming information that gives predators unrestricted access." He goes on to ask about your daughter's bedroom door. Does it have a lock? Most likely your answer is *Yes*. Every young lady needs a place of privacy where she can escape. If you are a good and considerate dad, you rightfully see yourself as giving her some privacy when she goes to her room and locks the door. But never forget this next part of Dr. Wolgemuth's warning: If she has her internet-based electronic device with her, then behind that very same door are millions of people — many of them men — doing their best to invade her privacy.[5]

How would you react if you saw a strange man trying to get past that locked door? I dare say I know the answer. How much more must we be ready to ward off the kind of men who slip into unlocked chat rooms seeking vulnerable teenage girls?

Who Are These Predators and How Do They Operate?

For an undramatized description of these men and their victims, I have turned to the double-published, oft-cited University of New Hampshire study "Online 'Predators' and Their Victims: Myths, Realities, and Implications for Prevention and Treatment." Published first in *American Psychology*, this article sheds a surprising light on many aspects of our daughters' online behaviors and the predators who are watching them, waiting for the right moment to enter that locked room.

Contrary to common thinking, it is not the posting of personal information that ranks highest for making an adolescent vulnerable to victimization. It is also not even "social media" per se. Instead, the real danger zones of the internet are the private, communication-oriented areas. Chat rooms, email, and private messaging are the places adults can hide as they seduce young girls into divulging themselves and developing romantic feelings. As Dr. Wolgemuth noted, it is the activity behind the locked door that we as parents need to monitor.

I am not talking about monitoring her time on the internet just because we think social media platforms are immoral or evil unto themselves. I am not even addressing the mush-brained laziness factor that too much surfing time has on your daughter's mind. Moreover, if you limit your daughter's electronic time because her grades are suffering, that sounds great. Just make sure your purpose is clear so she does not think you are worried about her soul. Even further, if you are afraid your daughter will somehow be targeted for abduction because of too many Instagram posts, your worries might not be grounded in the most current police statistics.

What we do want to worry about is whether our daughters are vulnerable to the predators online who know how to isolate them, make them feel comfortable disclosing intimate details about themselves, and eventually schedule a face-to-face encounter to consummate their relationship. With the sober reality of this secret world sinking in, please consider the following things to worry less about while heightening our awareness for more *blatant signs of trouble.*[6]

Worry Less ... Watch More

- Don't worry so much about her posting personal information online ... Rather, watch for *personal information being shared privately*! Online is honest and open. Private communication presents trouble!
- Don't worry so much about having unknown people as "followers" or even when your daughter "follows" someone she doesn't know personally ... Rather, watch for actual *mentions of sex and flirtations with unknown people.* "Following" someone is normal and expected in the youth culture today. Sexual innuendos with strangers imply something is off base.
- Don't worry so much about her watching hours and hours of random people's funny content ... Rather, watch for *downloading items from file-sharing programs.* You should be in tune with your daughter's file-sharing

programs! (e.g., Google Drive, Dropbox, LimeWire, eMule, KaZaa, etc.)

- Don't worry about exposure to culturally normal, sexually explicit ads and memes (you and I have been watching beer commercials and movies with love scenes all our lives, and we are okay) … Rather, watch for *deliberate visits to X-rated sites*. Pornography won't be mentioned much in this book except to say that we live in a world of it in various forms and levels, but when young girls begin visiting porn sites, something has gone awry and could lead to real vulnerability.

Don't let the following statistic make you lazy, but the number of teens who show these genuine signs of vulnerability to seduction from online predators is about 15%. That number might have changed since the publishing of this University of New Hampshire study, but even so, 15% is a low number. The rest of the teens online are just having normal, adolescent fun.[7]

We have all seen those TV shows, the ones where actors or someone in law enforcement poses as someone else online to prove to parents that their children are more susceptible to deception than the parents might want to believe. These shows are always eye-opening, but we need to realize that without any of the alarming behaviors above, our daughters are far less susceptible to becoming victims. As a matter of fact, "deception" is not usually a priority in a cyber-predator's *modus operandi* because if they can identify the prime girls with these online behaviors, they know they do not need as much deception. Their target—your daughter—has already signaled that she wants to be sought.[8]

That brings us, then, to wonder what we can do to prevent some of the behaviors above, especially when the very nature of these behaviors is so often hidden from open view. Like I said earlier, we could all just come down hard on our daughters with unyielding restrictions on their internet usage, but I never tried that. On a conceptual level, tough restrictions seemed pointless and ineffective to me.

That is not to say I stayed out of the fight, though. On the contrary, instead of fighting the internet, I decided to fight the vulnerabilities in my daughters. I did what I could to keep my daughters off the list of underlying characteristics that most likely lead to the behaviors above. The next section summarizes the most common traits, as discussed with evidence in the "Online 'Predators' and Their Victims" article. None of these characteristics can be avoided or eradicated altogether, but our goal as parents can be to reduce them to a level less damaging to our daughters' online integrity.

What Are These Vulnerabilities?

First, the most vulnerable adolescent girls see themselves as "alienated from and in conflict with their parents."[9] You may say, "Well, that's all teenage girls." Maybe so, but remember, all we can do is get our girls into the best spot possible. Do not accept the idea that your teenager is obligated by nature to feel perpetually alienated and in conflict with you. It is not true.

Next, most girls who prove to be vulnerable have a real "struggle with social interaction problems."[10] Social anxiety and getting along with others are real issues. The next chapter explores communication in-depth and shows us dads how to be proactive in helping our girls operate better in social settings, but for now, we must be aware of her levels of social distress. They can be signs of vulnerability.

Another vulnerability measure identifies those girls with the least understanding of the legal, health, and future sexual-development ramifications of early sexual experimentation. Do you know how many teenagers still do not know that they will be labeled a "sex offender" for life if they are caught hitting "send" on a naked photo of themselves or someone else?! Even more shocking is the ignorance among teens about STDs like HPV, one which causes cervical cancer and against which condoms have not proven effective.[11] When girls are less ignorant of legal and health-related realities, they become less vulnerable to victimization.

Finally, in addition to these characteristics, the most vulnerable girls are also more likely to be the girls who feel isolated in their own sexual feelings with no adults around who seem to understand what they are feeling. Again, dads can beat this feeling of isolation by being real with their daughters about the common sexual thoughts and feelings we *all* experience, not just in our adolescence.

As you reread and study this list of character traits that could make your daughter vulnerable, remember we are not talking about her being abducted in an old white van while jogging in the park. Rather, we are talking about her susceptibility to a grown man in a chat room who is seeking a consensual sexual relationship with an adolescent girl whom he can seduce into meeting him and even committing her emotions to him and their secrecy. The "set of skills" it takes to beat this guy is not the special ops training that made Bryan Wells able to track and kill his daughter's abductors. It is the set of skills I pray this book offers you.

How ironic is it that online predators, according to this same study in *American Psychologist,* "are patient enough to develop relationships with victims and savvy enough to move those relationships offline"?[12] How is it that these predators "know what to say to teens to gain their trust, arouse their sexual interest, and maintain relationships through face-to-face meetings"?[13] The irony is that if dads (and moms) could find the patience and savviness to develop relationships with their daughters and know what to say to gain their teens' trust and be embarrassingly honest about sexually explicit feelings going on in everyone's lives right now, then our daughters would not have the slightest need to share their intimate feelings with a new friend online who is old enough and mature enough to "understand them."

Your daughter's need for privacy is real, but do not let her private moments lead to your worst nightmare.

I asked a friend what his mindset was about "privacy" and like-matters when raising his three daughters. Tom's daughters are exemplary young ladies any dad would be proud of. His answer was simple. Everyone in his home had the right to their own privacy, but they understood their privacy only went so far. To make his point with his girls, he included himself. He would often remind his daughters, "Girls, you know my screen-lock password and you can use my phone/devices for whatever you need. You can see anything on my device at any time without even warning me first."

This openness from dad to daughters ensured the reciprocal openness which would be necessary for Tom to protect his girls from predators and pitfalls.

Emotional Battering and Drainage

I hope that is enough said about predators and physical danger because we need to move on to further threats that we as dads can watch for. The numbers of victims in this next area are far greater than the numbers we just covered. Whereas potentially 15% of girls using the internet will be approached by an online predator, almost 100% deal with emotional attacks every day.

I have titled this section "Emotional Battering and Drainage," and maybe I will point a finger at us dads a little for the part we play in it, but I don't want the accusation to be misconstrued as "Emotional Abuse." There is a difference. I hope you would not abuse your daughter emotionally. If you are prone to do so, find some help to beat your anger and your desire to put people under yourself. There are strategies you can implement to get a good handle on these things.

That is enough about that. What I prefer to call attention to is the amount of emotional battering and drainage your daughter endures on a regular basis and how you as a dad can do two things: 1) make sure you are not a part of the problem and 2) help her protect herself and heal from the treatment of others.

Find Your Own Pause Button

Sometimes girls might need a good lecture. As you can imagine from how many words I have flung around in this book so far, I have probably done my fair share of lecturing. However, I have learned through the worn-out look on my daughters' drained countenances that lecturing can do more harm than good. Your daughter's psyche can only handle so much lecturing before she begins to batten down the hatches and keep you out. I know this sounds cliché, but sometimes what your daughter needs is a hug, and an ounce of lecturing can erase a pound of concerned hugging.

Turn that lecture volume up with a raised tone of voice and a red face, and suddenly you are not only erasing all your previous hugs but now you are becoming a part of the emotional battering that *Dad, Security Detail* is supposed to protect her from. Obviously, kids need to hear some lecturing, but we dads need a keen sense of timing and appropriateness of emotion when our long power-point presentations get started.

We also need to know where our own pause button is so our daughters can talk. Your daughter needs to talk as much as you need her to listen. Besides that, she needs you to listen far more than you need to talk! I am not minimizing the power of your corrective words and the practicality of your foolproof solution to her problems. I am simply saying you and I need to keep our pause buttons handy. Your daughter needs you to pause long enough for her to interject. She needs permission to express herself to you, especially if she is in emotional pain.

Let Her Cry

I suppose I am rather stoical when it comes to emotional pain. That is not always good. One day my daughter's eyes welled with tears as she muttered a brave request of me, "Daddy, can I cry about this?"

I do not remember what she needed to cry about, but I learned that day my daughter needs to express her emotions. I suppose I had stressed to her up to that point the importance of being "tough." I am glad she was tough enough to cry that day. It taught me a lesson about the difference between her emotional pain and mine. Never again did I want my girls to feel like they were not allowed to tell me how they feel.

Watch the Criticism

One more thing I have had to learn to pause is my tendency toward criticism. I am brilliant when it comes to finding fault in others. I am so good at it, I wonder why I'm not rich. But when it comes to my daughters, I learned early on to see myself as their advocate rather than their accuser.

The effect of criticism in our lives is uncanny. I find it a wonder how our brain holds a lifetime of good memories within its mysterious folds, but the few things that stick out to us—even when we try to suppress them—are the criticisms we have received from others, especially from our parents. Parents excuse themselves by labeling their criticisms "constructive," but no matter what we call it, criticism stings. Even after good results arise from the criticism, the one who was critiqued deals with the sting for a long time to come.

Please do not peg me as an eggshell walker who tiptoes around my daughters' feelings. That is not what I am advocating, and if you ask my girls, they will tell you we deal with problems straight on at our house. We do not skirt issues just to save feelings, but we are careful with criticism because every critical word adds to the emotional battering and drainage our daughters already have to endure.

Be Angry, but Be Careful

I would be the last one to say you are not allowed to be angry with your daughter. Everyone gets angry, but as much as we are free to be angry when anger is due, ugliness is never due! One time, I had to clarify this to someone who misunderstood my honest confession of the open-borders approach to emotional expression we have in our home. Because I had told him we fight with each other until we reach a resolution, he thought I was excusing his ugliness toward his wife and kids. Anger is one thing; ugliness is another.

Be careful because the look and the sound of anger are always uglier than you realize. In our household, every one of us has said to the other at one time or other, "I wish you could hear and see yourself right now. You think you are just expressing your view, but you are borderline ballistic, and you don't even realize it."

Ugliness includes, but is not limited to, using foul language against each other and wounding each other with castigations that have nothing to do with the subject at hand. I am sure a discussion of ugliness in all its forms would be helpful here, but suffice it to say anger doesn't need ugliness to get its point across.

To be honest, I am usually the one pushing the limits of anger, but that does not make it right. These girls are not only my daughters; they are God's daughters too (and for that matter, my wife is God's daughter). If I were God and I walked in on Brian (me) yelling at My daughters in anger, I believe I might have something to say about it, and it would not be a fun experience for little Brian. It would not take Brian long to discover another approach to communicating and to take on the role of protector and healer rather than the angry dad.

We dads are supposed to heal our daughters of their emotional pains or at least lead them to their healing. The emotional battering our daughters endure throughout the day is daunting. For a little one, every conversation on the playground can lead to hurt feelings. Interactions with teachers and others in authority can leave our daughters with open wounds. Let boys enter the equation, and it can all go out of balance. Add to that your daughter's girl-friends' drama, which she has had to listen to all day in or-der to be the shoulder others cry on, and by the time she gets home in the evening, the emotional drainage has taken its toll.

These are the issues we need to hear about from our daughters so we can teach them to navigate their feelings and be the tough-skinned, soft-hearted people we want them to become.

Now I Know the Threats, but How Do I Protect Her?

To get her to the place where her heart is still soft but her skin is tougher, *Dad, Security Detail* has to be as proactive on the side of protecting her as he was when he first baby-proofed his home. He must prove vigilant and mind some proven strategies.

The strategies woven throughout this chapter so far should help, but there are a few more I have found worthy of offering to you, so I would like to conclude this chapter with some the approaches my wife and I took to guard our home and our daughters from physical, emotional, and emergency dangers; to shield our girls from personal ignorance and boy-related dangers; and to acclimate them to the character that counteracts the vulnerable behaviors of online victims.

#1. "Guard Your Heart" (She Has to Watch Out for Herself)

For starters, we emphasized to them that they are responsible for their own body, mind, and soul. We had one guiding scripture in our home regarding this principle: "Above all else, guard your heart, for everything you do flows from it" (Proverbs 4:23 NIV). We reminded them of it all the time and often posed it as a question for any emotional situations they were facing: "Were you guarding your heart?" This concept covers all their relationships. If ever their feelings were hurt or they seemed offended by another person's actions, we asked if they had been guarding their hearts. If one of them came home feeling vulnerable to someone else's opinion or to the whims of their peers, we asked, "Were you guarding your heart during that conversation?"

It is a principle your girl will keep for the rest of her life. To shield herself from wearing her heart on her sleeve, to filter her world through an optimistic lens, to select her own susceptibilities with great care … these are skills your daughter's peers may never discover, but if you teach her to guard her own heart, she will be much safer from all of the threats we have talked about.

#2. Opportunities to Learn (Experience Matters)

Another protection we offered our girls was the opportunity to be in specific social situations and test their skills. We started our girls early in Sunday School and children's church (not exactly for theology but rather for the benefits of social connection). As our girls grew, we allowed them to have sleepovers and stay over with friends (whose families we had vetted to the best of our intuitive abilities). When they were pre-teens and beyond, we sent them on trips with others, whether trips with a purpose organized by a local ministry or trips for fun just with another neighborhood family. As they grew older, we made sure they participated in extracurricular activities that put them right in the fray of social interaction.

All of these suggestions might sound counterintuitive to you, as if I have forgotten that every place I just mentioned is also where our girls could find themselves most vulnerable instead of protected, but that is the paradox of the cure. Vaccinations only work because they introduce enough of the disease to give your immune system a heads up. Putting our daughters in the middle of social situations helped them develop the skills that would keep them off the list of most likely victims.

#3. Where Are You, Baby? (GPS for Safety)

The next safeguard we used always struck a little chord of controversy with other people's views of personal freedom, but I always found their objections to this practice were due to a 100% misplacement of motive in their evaluation of us.

When we mention to others that our family *always* uses the GPS features of our phones to know each other's whereabouts at all times, their reactions are usually, "What? Don't you trust each other? That would *never* work with my daughter. She has to know I trust her!" These folks have no idea that a lack of trust never even crossed our radar when we put this into practice.

To us, it seems obvious that the best way to be on the ready to help each other and grant each other peace of mind is to share our GPS data. So sorry, naysayers, but I love opening my phone to see my daughters' profile pictures pinned to their locations wherever they happen to be on this planet. And my daughters love the fact that Daddy sees where they are. It is not about trust; it is about wearing the hat of *Dad, Security Detail*.

You might feel like what I am about to share is overkill, but we even had a rule in our home to text each other if there were changes to our plans or location. If one of our girls was scheduled to be at a dance, for instance, but instead of staying at the dance all her friends decided to hang out at Whataburger, she was required to send a simple text telling us of the change. The girls soon learned that texting us their details would lead to more freedom for themselves.

I do not care if she goes to Whataburger instead of a dance; what I care about is that I know where she is. Every moment of transition is critical if an emergency arises. Even if it were not a matter of "changing plans," our girls would still have to text their transitions. When leaving a sporting event and heading to an afterparty, they would text, "Leaving x" and "arrived at z."

One of our daughters had a job where she routinely clocked out near midnight and walked to her car alone. If this had not been a legitimate job, we would have been violating the local curfew ordinance for 16-year-old driving hours, so you better believe this dad wanted to know when his daughter's car was pointed toward home—with the doors locked.

As I said, this rule might sound like overkill to you, but in practice, it was quite simple. It *never* backfired in any negative way for our daughters or for us. On the contrary, it gave us peace of mind and widened the gates for our girls to spend time where they wanted to be. We were never looking over their shoulder in an intrusive way.

#4. Safeguard Today ... Point to Tomorrow

I think it is interesting that even Jesus' parents put restrictions on him to guide his social development. They worked within specific time frames for allowing him to experience different elements of growing up (see Luke 2). Mary and Joseph must have been great parents. I hope they would approve of the next strategy we found useful to protect our daughters. We will call this strategy "Safeguard Today by Pointing to Tomorrow."

We found it helpful to let our girls know that when they reached a certain age, certain boundaries would be stretched regarding their rights and responsibilities. A silly example that had nothing to do with keeping our girls safe was the Nobody-in-this-house-opens-the-refrigerator-until-they-are-10-years-old Rule. Silly as it was, it demonstrates the point. Besides the fact that it saved me a lot of electricity, my girls learned that if they have a moment in the future where certain experiences are guaranteed to come open to them, they are quite capable of placing their desires in the hope chest of a specific future time and place.

It also provided four priceless memories in our home. The day each of our girls turned 10, the first thing they did was head to the kitchen and open the refrigerator door, staring mindlessly at the food just like a grown-up!

This tactic will prove useful with so many more serious issues your girls will want to experience but will be willing to postpone as long as they understand when the reins are going to be loosened. If you cannot provide honest dates for your daughter when implementing this strategy, just call it the I'm-Not-Sure-When-But-You-Will-Eventually-Get-To Coping Mechanism: "One day, daughter, a whole new set of emotions and physical experiences will be opened to you … I promise. But 14 years old is not the age for that."

Be specific with your promises. If it has to do with her physical desires to be with a boy, then be specific about when such touching and experimenting will become a part of her world. Learning to postpone her desires is doable; being told her desires are taboo and that she just should not want those things is dangerous.

#5. Safe Haven

Finally, *Dad, Security Detail* can perform many of his duties simply by prioritizing home as a "Safe Haven." Where is your daughter's safe haven? Pay close attention to where she gravitates. If she does not gravitate toward home, ask yourself what can be done to re-mark the boundaries and make her feel safe.

Our home has always been the place where our girls were the freest to be themselves and make their mistakes. As a personal choice, we have not used our home for too many "outreach opportunities." If your philosophy is different from ours and your home has a revolving door for needy guests, maybe you can think of a place within your home or connected to your family (Grandma's house maybe?) where your daughter knows she doesn't have to worry about "guests" barging in on her or even eavesdropping. This might not even be something you deal with in your world, but if it is, try whatever you can to establish a safe haven for your daughter. She will feel protected and she will credit you for the protection detail.

The Conclusion of the Matter: Speak to Her Heart

One of the hardest challenges concerning everything we have discussed so far will be convincing your daughter in her heart of hearts that the safeguards you implement in your household routines and family structure are genuinely for her benefit. That is where your dad-skills of communication come into play, and that is where we will turn our attention next. Not only do we need to communicate our own purposes clearly, but we also must show our daughters the dignity and strength they will gain by learning the best ways to *communicate*.

Head to the hat rack, *Dad, Security Detail*. It is time to try on a new hat: *Dad, Communications Director*.

[1] Jesus, Gospel of Matthew 13:44-46

[2] McManners, Hugh. *The Complete Wilderness Training Manual*. Metro Books, an Imprint of Sterling Publishing Co., Inc., 2015.

[3] "Sex Offender Registry/Search." *RecordsFinder*, 26 April 2020, recordsfinder.com/sex-offenders/.

[4] Welborn, Vickie. "Show Features Justin Bloxom Murder." *Shreveporttimes.com*, 30 Mar. 2015, www.shreveporttimes.com/story/news/local/2015/03/30/justin-bloxom-investigation-discovery-amy-fletcher-brian-horn-murder-desoto-parish-dustin-rosegrant-adam-ewing-keith-banta/70695842/.

[5] Wolgemuth, Robert D. *She Calls Me Daddy: 7 Things You Need to Know about Building a Complete Daughter*. Tyndale House Publishers, Inc., 2014.

[6] Wolak, Janis, et al. "Online 'Predators' and Their Victims: Myths, Realities, and Implications for Prevention and Treatment." *American Psychologist*, vol. 63, no. 2, 2008, pp. 111–128., doi:10.1037/0003-066x.63.2.111.

[7] Ibid., 123

[8] Ibid., 117

[9] Ibid., p. 123

[10] Ibid., p. 123

[11] Manhart, Lisa E., and Laura A. Koutsky. "Do Condoms Prevent Genital HPV Infection, External Genital Warts, or Cervical Neoplasia?" *Sexually Transmitted Diseases*, vol. 29, no. 11, 2002, pp. 725–735., doi:10.1097/00007435-200211000-00018.

[12] Wolak, p. 119

[13] Ibid., p. 119

3

Dad, Communications Director

Ok, so I have a degree in Communications, but that does not make me much more expert at communicating than anyone else who has also lived their whole lives having to get along with all these crazy people down here on planet Earth. All of us must learn to communicate. Some might be quicker learners than others, but everyone can learn to communicate in a way that works for them and enhances their relationships.

For your daughter, I bet talking comes easy. Statistically speaking, she probably churns out more words in an hour than you do in three days, but talking does not necessarily equal communicating, so it is our responsibility to help our daughters see the difference. If you are willing to get serious with your daughter's potential as a power-communicator, this chapter will get you started.

In the last chapter, we talked about guarding our daughters' lives and limbs, keeping them safe right down to their hearts, but now we want to teach them to guard the one part of themselves that can make or break them in this world ... their mouths. As much as your girl needs her daddy for *security detail*, she needs him even more to be *Dad, Communications Director*.

Start with Listening

In the middle of the last chapter, we touched on the importance of listening. Many people do not realize that listening is the first line of communicating and that listening skills can be taught. Learning to listen is the first lesson you will want to cover when teaching your daughter to be a good communicator, but the way to teach it best is to listen to her. We must show our daughters that we are good listeners. It might not be something you perfect, but it is definitely something you pursue.

How do you know you are a good listener? First, do you have any clue what your daughter just said? When you were together last, did you lock in on her or were you in a different world while her mouth was moving? No matter how old your daughter is right now, I promise you, she knows better than you do whether you are listening, and from watching you, she is learning how to listen.

When we listen, there are signs to prove it. We lean in toward the speaker. We make appropriate gestures of interest like a slight move of the eyebrows, a crinkling of the nose, or a contortion of the lips. We interject with questions, both for clarification and for gleaning extra details. We restate what we have heard to reassure the speaker we are onboard. We look into the speaker's eyes.

We listen with our eyes as much as our ears. If our eyes are looking past the speaker into space, we have no idea what her subtle implications might be. *Oh, wait, was she just kidding or was she serious? I have no clue because I was not listening with my eyes.* Besides that, the space-stare also says, "I'm not even in this room with you. Tap me when you're done so I can grunt and nod." These are just a sample of the cues we offer to show we are listening. It does not take a genius to read these signs.

It does take a genius, however, to check himself for these signs. Are you willing as a dad to make some genius moves? Can you ignore the TV in the background while your little girl tells you about her craft project at school? Can you avoid your cellphone on purpose so your eight-year-old daughter knows how it feels to be someone's priority? Can you close the ledger on your desk, with its worrisome red digits pressuring you to make another dollar, so your sophomore girl can tell you how she was selected to represent her school at a really cool summit?

Becoming a genius listener takes putting things on hold, even if it's your buddy the president calling for advice on a foreign affairs dilemma: "Excuse me, Mr. President. I will be with you in a minute. My daughter is in the middle of a story." Indeed, putting things on hold to listen attentively does not come naturally. If you are like me, listening intently almost hurts, but you do it anyway. You do not see it as an inconvenient chore; it is more like a genius-level DIY project.

The point of all this listening, remember, is to teach your daughter the first lesson of good communication: being a good listener. You start teaching her by showing her yourself. Then you begin to expect her to be a listener too.

Now, Let's Communicate

Besides listening, there are levels and levels of interpersonal communication you can dive into with your daughter. The skills you equip your girl with over the time you have her in your home will pave the way for her destiny.

My old college Interpersonal Communication textbook claims, "The quality of your existence is directly linked to the quality of your communication."[1] I have to agree with that.

Indeed, communication will be the key to success in almost every area of her life. Research shows that communication skills are directly related to relationship satisfaction.[2] In other words, the level of your daughter's future happiness in relationships will be the effect of how well she learns to communicate under your watch. Moreover, if your daughter lands that dream job in her chosen career, it will most likely be because she killed the face-to-face interview. She has to know how to break the ice, keep the conversation going, and get out while the getting is good.

Finally, I could not leave these introductory thoughts alone without referencing a harsh life-or-death-sized warning from one of the leading researchers regarding the links between social happiness and your physical well-being. James J. Lynch, author of *The Language of the Heart: The Body's Response to Human Dialogue*, put a seal on the importance of learning to communicate when he revealed that the entire body is subject to the quality of your communication. How? … because dialogue has a direct effect on the cardiovascular system.[3] He clinches his warning by insisting that to ignore the importance of communication is to "increase our chances of prematurely dying alone."[4]

Wow. That puts a heavy responsibility on you, *Dad, Communications Director*.

Learning to live together means learning to communicate, and that is something dads can teach their daughters. Whether it's as simple as walking her through how to introduce herself to a new friend or as complicated as teaching her how to tell a funny story, you can help your daughter in practical ways become a great communicator. From learning the best way to insert herself into a conversation to how to exit an uncomfortable moment, your girl will benefit from any advice you can give.

You do not have to be an expert. None of us are. Maybe you can just be willing to learn the ropes with her. It is a matter of being purposeful about it. If, for instance, you find yourselves in a moment where an apology is needed — maybe from her to a sibling or a friend — you can take time to help her word the apology in a way that genuinely accepts blame and asks for forgiveness.

Or let's say she is struggling with what to say in a very important text which the recipient will read repeatedly with every possible inflection. If you and she are used to batting communication ideas off each other, she will know she can come to you for the best wording. All of these types of personal interactions are things people should have the privilege of learning at home. Too many people enter adulthood ill-prepared to face the fear-inducing world of communicating.

Maybe you feel ill-prepared yourself. Take heart. In the next few pages, I want to take you through some specific examples of ways to teach her to communicate. I have done my best to provide some real-life scenarios to prepare her for — like delivering arguments, forming apologies, and learning to introduce herself — but there is no way I can cover every situation she will face.

Before we get to those common circumstances, however, I will let you in on some of the secret methods I employed to get the lessons into my daughters' psyches. Instead of sitting around wracking my brain to write out lesson plans, I usually relied on one of these Simple Teaching Moments.

Simple Teaching Moments

#1. Prayer

Most of the time, instead of trying to create a scenario from which to teach, if I knew there was an issue one of my girls needed to work on, I would pray for the opportunity to arise on its own. Yes, I just said *Prayer* is my first secret weapon. I do not know how you feel about prayer, but these are the kinds of prayers God seems to answer best. Within only a short time after such a prayer for my daughter, suddenly I would find myself with my foot in my mouth and be able to use my own misstep as a perfect example for my daughter to learn what not to say in a given situation. Then I am sure God would have a laugh at my expense.

Laughing aside, I hope you will give prayer a real chance as a Teaching Moment producer. When you notice a pattern in your daughter's communication problems and take just a moment to mention them in prayer, I promise within the next few days or even minutes, a "coincidence" will suddenly open the door to a discussion you could not have made happen on your own.

Maybe you could have made it happen on your own but not without making both you and your daughter uncomfortable. I cannot tell you how many times I specifically talked to God about an issue my daughters were dealing with. I don't have statistics to prove it, but I think God — and prayer—made a big difference in how my daughters learned to communicate their thoughts and feelings to me, their mom, and their world.

#2. Prep-Talk Pep-Talks

Another secret way I would get communication lessons across to my daughters was through *Prep-talk Pep-talks*. If we were headed into a social setting—say, a wedding or a neighborhood party, for example—we would take just a minute to run through the most likely scenarios that could arise. I might tell her to make sure she greets certain people before going off to do her own thing or to make sure she is prepared to be nice to someone who normally rubs her the wrong way.

These kinds of prep-talks can happen like a huddle in the car just before exiting. They are quick and easy, but they make a world of difference. If you just think ahead a half-second, you will predict things about where she is heading that unfold for her exactly as you said. For just an extra moment of purposeful coaching, you will look like a prophet in your daughter's eyes.

If you are privileged to be the drop-off parent on school days, you use the last minute of the drop to remind her what to say to the person who has been giving her trouble in class or maybe how to square her body language off like a champion. Dropping her off for softball practice, you remind her how to approach her coach. Taking her across town to her babysitting job, you cover little reminders about how children communicate. I am just throwing out a few examples so you can see that they are endless.

We are not talking about long lectures; anytime you have a brief window to give your girl a heads up on what is coming her way, you will be moving one step closer to being *Dad, Communications Director*.

#3. Post-Talk

Then there is the secret tool of the *Post-talk* strategy, taking time to review a social experience after you leave. Post-talks are composed of a quick recap of how she did in a situation or maybe something you and she noticed together that would have worked better.

Post-talks can be fruitful for several reasons. If you can avoid a critical, corrective tone as much as possible, instant feedback will capitalize on the feelings and immediate memory of the moment. Feedback does not always have to be about errors you noticed in her behavior; post-talk can serve your purposes even better when used to praise her for words well-spoken or for the self-restraint she displayed in a tough social setting. If positive recapping moments become a regular part of your relationship, you might be amazed at how much she opens up to you.

Conversely, sitting in the back of your SUV on a long ride home after dealing with a trying social confrontation will lead only to a pent-up existence of self-brooding. Her little heart will be discombobulated, and you do not even realize it because you did not have a post-talk. That is where a lot of little girls live because they do not learn to talk about where they just came from. However, get your daughter in the habit of post-talks and you will not need the radio on your drive home.

Post-talk might also be useful because it provides your daughter a chance to get her gossip-need settled in a constructive way. I am kidding; gossip is wrong. However, there is something special about the father-daughter bonding that happens when you laugh together because So-n-So was so off-base to say such-n-such about la-dee-dah, and you can't believe Mrs. Blah Blah rolled her eyes when Mr. Blah Blah left the room. Haha, ok, we *were* gossiping ... Sorry. At least we were on the same page, though. Post-talk is good for that.

#4. Do-Over

When you are not in the middle of a social situation but rather talking things over within the privacy of the family, you can always use what we will call the *Do-over* strategy. A bonus feature of this strategy is the forgiveness and patience it encourages, as it is built on the premise that sometimes it is okay to take your words back and try to say them better.

In our house, when our girls said something a little less respectful than was called for, we would often let them have a do-over. Okay, okay ... even more often, we would go a full three rounds fighting it out, but if we ever stopped long enough to be rational, we would offer a do-over. We might even brainstorm the top three better ways something could have been said. Getting to say things over, having to repeat thoughts out loud, and considering alternative wording are great lessons in getting along. Facilitating a deliberate do-over teaches your girl how to communicate clearly and how to say exactly what she means to say.

#5. Pause-It

Finally, the secret weapon my girls probably hated the most but which I had the most fun with is the *Pause-it* strategy. This would happen while we were watching a TV show or movie. For the record, I hate interruptions during a movie, but for this method, I interrupted things all the time. I would pause a movie when one of the characters said something I thought should be analyzed and applied to our communication skills: "See, Girls, *that's* what happens when you say something *that* way!" It sounds silly, but I think it worked.

We did not stop for long discussions or stay up all night just to get through a movie, but I would take advantage of any moment that jumped out to me as a chance to learn how to be a more responsible communicator. Think of all the moments in this life you can pause just long enough to let them soak in. If you think a moment will help you teach your girl, do not let it play to the next scene. The Pause-it strategy is a great way to learn.

"Pause-it," "Do-over," "Post-talk," "Prep-talk Pep-talk," and Prayer: that is about it. That exhausts my cache of skills as *Dad, Communications Director*, but the types of circumstance these secret methods enhanced were endless. The following section provides a brief list of common social scenarios where you and your daughter might team up to implement these communications tools and let her become the great communicator she is destined to be. I hope each one has enough hands-on details for you to find them useful.

Social Scenarios: Daughter in Training

Initiating Introductions

She Calls Me Daddy covers introductions in a section called "It's nice to meet you, Dr. Holland." In this section, Dr. Wolgemuth recounts how his daughters were required to introduce themselves if they happened to run into one of their daddy's friends or acquaintances while they were out and about. He would make sure his daughter made eye contact, extended her hand, and spoke in a firm, kind tone. I thought this was a great exercise for teaching your girl how to introduce herself to others.

When our family dealt with this uncomfortable necessity of learning to break the ice by initiating personal introductions, I drilled my girls with a principle laden with reverse psychology. The principle is that beautiful people are not afforded the right to be shy. "If a beautiful girl is shy," I would say to my girls, "people do not see it as shyness ... instead, they will label her a snob!"

As much as I said this in our home, my girls grew tired of hearing it, but the principle served its double purpose: a) it told my girls that I considered them a "beautiful" girl, and b) it forced them to be the first to introduce themselves so they would not be thought a snob. Snobbery was harder to bear than the difficulty of initiating an introduction.

Polite Interruptions[5]

When our daughters were very little, we had simple rules about whether it is appropriate to interrupt others, especially adults. The rule was if you or someone else is bleeding and you can't get the tourniquet tight enough, then say, "Excuse me, Daddy or Mommy, I am sorry to interrupt, but we have an emergency." For everything else, you can wait.

You will be glad to know that was an exaggeration, but there is some truth in it. Interruptions are rude if they are not dire, so our children need to learn how to perform them politely. My daughters have honored us so well that if they do interrupt, we know we need to stop what we are doing in order to listen.

I suppose the art of making interruptions comes down to a mindset. Teach your daughter about humility (not sheepishness, but the humility which starts with "I am sorry to interrupt" and is quick to deliver its message). Teach her that direct, explanatory words are a better attention-getter than tugging on your shirt or standing behind your guest flailing her arms. Teach her that she is important enough to be able to interrupt and wise enough to know when it is appropriate. Since you are not the only person she will have to interrupt in her life, she needs to know how to do it wisely.

Storytelling and Humor

I cannot tell you how many hours of moment-for-moment, detailed, super-long stories I have endured along the path of preparing my girls to become good storytellers. Sadly, if you are ever going to get that chance, then you, too, will have to let your girl talk on and on. Once she knows how much you value her long, drawn-out stories, she will be more inclined to listen when you coach her on getting to the bottom line. It is important to get her to the bottom line, though, because if she puts her friends through long nights of unnecessary details, she will not have her friends for too long.

Telling a story succinctly means thinking it through quickly before you start. Teach your daughter to include four elements in the retelling of her day: *a setting, a quick plot, an endpoint, and a reason for telling it*. If she can see herself hitting these markers, she will waste fewer words and become quite entertaining, which will make her feel special as a communicator.

Of course, if she wants to tell her story, she will probably want to make people laugh too. That means you need to help her with a few standards for humor. Early on, I taught my girls the ones that can be taught. The ones that cannot be taught without a whole drama department at your disposal are the subtleties of timing, slapstick, and rhetoric. However, the parts which can be taught are important for keeping her friends and building relationships, one of the subtle points of this whole communication chapter.

Teach your daughter that the best comics follow several basic no-no's: 1) never make fun of someone's looks, 2) never attack someone else's personal tastes, and 3) never speak lightly of other's unalterable traits or circumstances. I cannot remember where I learned these myself, so I cannot properly cite them, but if you can figure these out and teach them to your daughter, she might rise up as a phenomenal comic.

If it seems facetious for me to include a humor lesson in this mini-manual of communication skills, let me clarify that humor is one of the most important features of our social interactions. Humor binds us together. It helps us face our uncomfortable moments and discuss difficult topics. Even when it pushes the envelope, humor is rooted in relatability. If humor breaks down, so does communication. Indeed, what your daughter laughs at and how she makes others laugh can make a world of difference in her ability to communicate, so while you are teaching her to talk, help her be funny too.

Texting, Messaging, Posting

Another important aspect that can dictate where your daughter's path takes her has been mentioned several times already: texting, messaging, and posting. I guess the days are gone when kids pass notes back and forth. Now what they do is send messages and tag each other in posts.

I understand why. For me, text messaging and Facebooking have become some of the most useful tools of my career. Nowadays, I lean so much on texting that I might forget to check my voicemail for days at a time. I even use my text threads and social media posts as record keepers and reminders. I have not been diagnosed by a doctor, but I am sure my thumbs have a touch of arthritis from texting too much. I just think texting is a brilliant way to communicate.

However, texting and posting have their downside. Since text does not include inflections of voice, a single message can be read in myriad ways. Because I know this, sometimes I will add a postscript to a text to say something like, "Please be sure to hear my voice when you read this. You have known me long enough to know I would not sound frustrated about this."

I am a grown man texting other adults, yet we can misread each other's texts and ruin a perfectly good day. How much more do you think your daughter is susceptible to the pitfalls of messaging and posting? She never actually talks on the phone, and her texting language is often abbreviated or acronymic beyond being recognizable as her native language. Because of this, you will need to be active in helping her learn to communicate through text.

You will remember from our chapter about protecting her from electronic predators that she does deserve some privacy, but she also needs to trust you enough to let you read her messages. No one should have anything to hide on their phone unless they are planning a surprise party for you.

One of my daughters reminded me when she saw me typing this that my wife and I never violated our girls' privacy by looking over their shoulders at their texts or social media posts. However, that was because we got an early start building trust within our relationships. If you need to be in your daughter's business, remember my friend Tom's trade-off with his daughters: "You can see my phone too."

Back to the point, though, we could all use a personal editor for our texting, and *Dad, Communications Director* is his daughter's editor-in-chief. In the previous chapter, we addressed the dangers to check for on your girls' electronic devices, but now let's just see about helping her be a better communicator.

It might not seem this way, but your daughter would love for you to approve of the wording in an important text before she hits "send." She would love for you to help her avoid confusion in her already shaky friendships. She would love for you to keep her from looking like a narcissist on her Instagram feed. If you could help her change just one word or put a comma in just the right place so her post says what she thinks it says, she would be happy to bring her phone to you. And you will be a happy dad who has gone to a brand-new level in his daughter's communication training.

Let me close this thought with one more reason a parent's job as message-editor is so important. In recent years, it has become common hiring practice among employers to deemphasize the traditional resume and instead scroll through an applicant's social media posts. Many callbacks never happen because young ladies must not have had a mom or dad who would edit the immaturity out of their social posts. Now, they are 25 and starting a career, but the doors are closing based on a permanent record of who they used to be.

Helping your daughter hone her texting and posting skills will move her to the front of the line. Take a chance and see if she would like your help.

Delivering Arguments

Now we come to a point in this book where I can claim plenty of experience! If my household had one identifying mark, I am a little ashamed to tell you it would be the amount of arguing we did every single day! If you can pride yourself on few arguments around your house, you are doing way better than I ever could. With my beautiful contrarian wife, it is hard to go a day without fighting (Just kidding, Baby. You are perfect). But seriously, six different personalities living under the same roof are bound to disagree with each other on occasion. That is why we had to learn the art of arguing.

One of my daughters just married an attorney who was a national debate champion in college, so she will thank me one day for the lessons she picked up in the battles of our home.

The first lesson for presenting an argument is to remember who you are arguing with. We had to learn in our home that we are *not* each other's enemies; we might not agree with each other, but we definitely want the best for each other. That is step one.

Step two has already been covered twice in this book, so I will leave it at this: Avoid ugliness. Ugliness is ugly.

Step three is to recognize the other person's position. Restate what you think they are saying. Listen to see if you have understood them correctly. If you find out you have been wrong, then quit. If you are right about what you think they think, then at least you have assigned them the dignity of understanding.

Finally, speak slowly and say all of what you need to say. You do not have to be eloquent, but get it all out. If someone interrupts you, come back to what you were saying. Getting your whole argument out is important for everyone.

These four steps will help your daughter feel prepared for presenting an argument. You might even help with the steps. For instance, you can close an argument with your daughter by encouraging Step 4: "Did you get to say everything you were thinking, Daughter? Is there anything you wanted to add but you felt cut-off from saying? When I am thinking about this later, I want to make sure your whole voice was heard." Lead her through her arguments; one day she will need this skill.

There is so much more to say regarding arguments in the home. If we teach our kids to follow these few steps, they might be able to minimize the interruptions and the yelling. I have great hopes that you can minimize these things in your home, but I have to be honest: we never vanquished interrupting and yelling from ours. However, our girls learned enough about arguing that when they are with non-family-members, they can represent their positions well. They are not afraid to enter a friendly debate or work out a compromise with a roommate because they learned how to deliver an argument at home.

Arguments are necessary for the existence of a free society, so your girl should learn to argue well, but at least two more precautions about arguing have served us well in our home. I would not want to close this section without touching on them.

First, arguments do not have to be "won." Sometimes the adage, "We'll agree to disagree" is the best resolution. Maybe you would disagree with me about this, but the downside of winning an argument is the feeling you get when the other person finally bows out. It never satisfies like you thought it was going to. This is the paradox which rules the underside of haggling: the winner can look and feel like a loser because he wound up on top. What a good reason to let arguments rest after you have followed the four steps above and said what you want to say.

The other unpleasant feature of arguing is similar. We called it "the yuckiness of the last word." I do not know how else to explain it, but as much as you think you want to have the last word in an argument, there is something unpleasant about it. Maybe we need the last jab because we want them to be shocked into an immediate agreement with us. But 99 out of 100 arguments never end with two people agreeing wholeheartedly on the issue. Rather, each party can only hope they have said enough to give the other something to think about.

If your daughter learns to express her side of an issue clearly, she can learn next to let it go. If the other person ever comes around to her point of view, it will most likely be because they went away and thought about it for themselves. Granting others the last word isn't granting consent to their argument; it is a demonstration of faith in the process, and it will keep your daughter from carrying around the yuckiness of having the last word.

Making Apologies

Talk about yuckiness! No one likes to apologize. We live in a world where people never learn the art of making a real apology, so we are surrounded by yuckiness. Your daughter will have some of the best relationships on earth if she learns to apologize well. Her coaches, teachers, bosses, and friends, future spouse, and children will all feel a positive connection with her if she can master just a couple of principles relating to making apologies.

Apologies are best when they are quick and authentic.

I suppose I should be careful here because my wife says my apologies come too quick. You see … I apologize to my wife as soon as I realize I am wrong, and when it comes to our personal arguments, sometimes I realize I am wrong the very moment she explains her viewpoint. When the epiphany hits me, I am ready to apologize and walk away, but she cannot believe I changed my mind so fast. In addition, she does not feel she even got rolling enough for me to have heard her fully. Therefore, we are required to argue a little longer until my grovel-timing becomes more appropriate.

I am sure an observer would laugh at some of the arguments between me and KaLyndia, but laughing aside, I think apologies should be made as quickly as possible.

They must also be authentic. No one appreciates an apology for what you "might" have done. If you were not wrong, then do not apologize, but if you were wrong, you need to make your apology authentic.

We taught our girls they were not allowed to say, "if" in an apology. They could not say, "I'm sorry *if* I hurt your feelings," "I'm sorry *if* you felt rejected," or "I'm sorry *if* I stayed out too late without texting to let you know what was going on." The word "if" in an apology has a subtle way of letting the speaker avoid actual fault and shift the blame. Literally, to say, "I'm sorry *if* that offended you" puts the onus on the one who took offense, not on you for saying whatever you said. Instead of "if," then, we taught our girls to say, "I am sorry *because* I should not have done what I did," or "I am sorry *for* saying what I said." There is a big difference between "if" and "because."

Keeping Confidentiality

A little-known difference-maker in successful interpersonal communication is the ability to keep a confidence. If you can teach your daughter how important it is to be someone's trusted confidante, she will never lack friends. Everyone she knows will consider her a best friend because she will be able to offer them something which is by-and-large absent from our society: trustworthiness. As *Dad, Communications Director*, you can instill the concept of confidentiality in her and teach her a few rules to safeguard her relationships.

Earlier, I made a joke about gossip, but in the real world—in your daughter's world—gossip is no joke. It wears a thousand masks, sneaking around looking for opportunities to instigate betrayal. If you would like your daughter to be a champion of confidentiality, you will need to make sure she never wears any of gossip's masks. I do not want to go into all the various masks, but "concern" is one of them. It might sound something like, "I'm not really gossiping; I'm just so concerned about Susie-Q. Do you know what she's going through with her boyfriend?" In religious circles, the mask might be called a "prayer request" and sound like, "Let's all remember to be praying for the Smiths. You know they're still dealing with that terrible moral issue." Trustworthy people can be concerned for you by themselves and pray for you in their own private closet. Your daughter will be loved by many if she proves herself trustworthy.

Early on in her life, you might also need to free her little mind from any burden to be a "tattletale." Tattletales gain points with grownups, but they are quickly pushed out of peer circles. Maybe the best way to teach your daughter not to be a tattletale is to let her know the types of behavior that *cannot* be kept secret. If she memorizes the list, then she will not struggle with the tattletale's presumed obligation to divulge friends' normal secrets.

Since this is such a sensitive subject, I want to bullet point the items no one should ever keep secret for anyone else. If your daughter knows these, she can stop a friend mid-sentence to warn them that the confidentiality of the moment is ending (her honesty could save her relationships and maybe even lives):

- A desire to commit self-harm or a confession of having done so
- Information that affects the well-being of a child, i.e., knowledge of any form of child abuse
- Information that affects the well-being of an adult who does not have the capacity to defend himself or herself, e.g., the elderly, people with disabilities, etc.
- Blatantly illegal activities

If you think more should be added to this list, go for it. The point is simply that if she is sure of the things you would expect her to tattletale about, then she can be free to offer confidentiality for everything else.

I am not trying to set your daughter up in her own counseling service. I am simply referring to a principle of friendship which only a few people ever grasp. If my friend does not specifically give me permission to spread the content of our conversations, then those conversations should be considered confidential.

It is funny how people will exclaim, "But I only told one other person!" as if that justifies their lack of trustworthiness. How is it not obvious that if everyone tells just one person, the whole campus will hear the story before the end of the day? If your daughter can hear something in private from one of her friends and be dog-determined not to tell even one other person, you will have placed your daughter in a rare position of trustworthiness among her friends.

I have four daughters. Each of them has tasted betrayal. All of them understand the importance of keeping their friends' private information private. As PKs (see chapter one for more on Preacher's Kids), they got a little head start on the importance of confidentiality. They knew growing up that Daddy plans to carry other people's stories to the grave. They saw me walk out of earshot from them if I received a phone call from someone whose business did not need to be known to my family. They heard me tell stories without using people's names or without giving up any identifying details. They also knew that they could trust me to keep their own information safe.

Here I am writing a book about it, but you know what I mean. Confidentiality is imperative to good relationships, and it can be taught.

Carrying a Conversation

My dad is a great conversationalist, but he does not think he is and has told me so. He once remarked that as much as he likes going to fun events (e.g., he and my mom are fabulous dancers), he does not like the idea of having to be in a "small talk" moment. He has done well anyway, but I can see the pride in his eyes when he sees that his granddaughters (my brother's daughters too) have broken the fear and can burst into conversation with anyone at any moment. Maybe girls come by the next principles naturally, but I thought we could cover them anyway as a closing to our communications briefing.

How can you help your girl know how to carry a conversation? Here are a few tips.

First, teach her to keep a few *questions* handy to break the ice. "Where are you from? What's it like there? How did you wind up at our school?" It's the old Who, What, Why, Where, and How. That is how conversations get started, and follow-up questions are how they keep moving along.

After that, teach her about *hooks*. Hooks reveal your involvement in the conversation, letting the other person see you are genuinely interested. A hook occurs when you use the same word someone else just used to link your next statement with theirs. Your girl can learn to listen for hooks that pique her own interest so she can parlay with anyone about anything.

Then there is the subtle conversation technique called *disclosure*. This is a little-known secret weapon of disarmament. It bespeaks relatability. Disclosure is the simple act of revealing something about your personal self: your thoughts, your experiences, your vulnerabilities. Studies have shown that using disclosure in a conversation helps others feel they know you as a person.[6] This can happen within minutes of meeting someone and can keep them interested in continuing the conversation with you.

And that leads to the final tip you can teach your girl about being a conversationalist. She needs to know how to *exit*. Of course, she could always pretend her phone is buzzing: "This is my dad! He will be soooo upset if I ignore his call." But there are other ways to make her escape with clear body language and verbal cues like, "It has been nice talking to you." Bringing a conversation to a close is a skill she really needs. For that matter, she also needs to pick up other's hints about needing to move on. You can teach her that too.

Speaking of Exits: Conclusion

Lining all these ideas out in a tidy little chapter about being *Dad, Communications Director* makes me sound as if I deliberately set out to teach each of these concepts to my daughters, setting them down in the living room with their notebooks and pens to make sure they knew everything there is to know about the subject of communication. That is not how it happened.

I do get a little teachy every now and then, but all the concepts in this chapter (and the whole book) evolved organically just by having these girls under our care for all these years. I have dug into my personal journals and memory to find the actual concepts I consistently thought about when helping my girls navigate their journeys and negotiate their successes. I did not line these ideas out as a plan before I got started. Rather, this book is a recap I hope younger fathers can use as a pre-cap. If your girl is old enough, maybe you can read these chapters together and talk about them.

Talking through them might make your job as her *Security Detail* and *Communications Director* flow a little more naturally. If it does, then you will be able to flow more naturally with the next hat because you are already wearing it: *Dad, her First Love.*

[1] Stewart, John Robert., et al. *Together: Communicating Interpersonally*. Roxbury Publ. Co., 2004. p.17

[2] Eğeci, İ.S., Gençöz, T. Factors Associated with Relationship Satisfaction: Importance of Communication Skills. *Contemp Fam Ther* 28, 383–391 (2006).

[3] Stewart, p. 18

[4] Lynch, James J. *The Broken Heart: The Medical Consequences of Loneliness*. Basic Books, 1979. p.14

[5] *She Calls Me Daddy* also includes great insight into teaching children how to interrupt.

[6] Stewart, John Robert., et al. *Together: Communicating Interpersonally*. Roxbury Publ. Co., 2004. p. 256

4

Dad, Her First Love

I have hedged all my parenting bets on this one ancient declaration: Love never fails. If my thoughts, actions, and words are motivated by love—if they are rooted in love—then my part in my relationships will not fail.

The passage where this declaration is found also outlines the divine characteristics of love.[1] This outline is the best way I have found to judge myself. If I respond to a person with patience and kindness, for instance, I know my compass is pointing true north because the passage says, "Love is patient and kind." If, on the other hand, I feel the pressure of envy or pride weighing on a relationship, I know my compass is failing and I have gotten off course because "love is never envious, boastful or proud." Love never dishonors others even if a disagreement arises. Love is not easily angered, even if a heightened response to someone else's behavior is justifiable and appropriate. If anger is appropriate, it will still feel like love; if it doesn't, then it isn't.

At least that is how I see it. If I find myself protecting myself or seeking only what would benefit me, I know I have abandoned true love. Love protects others, makes itself vulnerable to others, hopes for the best in others, and perseveres when others let it down. Like the ancient passage says, "Love never fails."

There's No Way Around It

This chapter is about love. This hat you are already wearing is *Dad, her First Love*. It says everything your daughter needs you to know about how she sees you. Please note it is not, "Dad *should* be her first love" or even, "She *wants* Dad to be her first love." No, in her eyes, you *are* her first love. In her heart, this is what it is.

How you deal with it will inform her evolution as a person more than you could ever imagine. Sure, she might meet many fatherly figures throughout her life who all help her in fatherly ways, but the title First Love will always be yours. So far in this book, we looked into being *Dad, Security Detail* and *Dad, Communications Director* because those positions will protect her and help her navigate the future successfully, but to be *Dad, her First Love* makes you the model by which she evaluates her relationships with all men.

I dare say how you play your role will even influence how she views God. I do not want to overplay my hand here, so I will pass without raising the pot any further, but the odds are in my favor: your daughter's First Love is reading this book right now, and he is the meter by which she measures the world. Right now, she loves you more than anything in the world, and she hopes you love her too.

Affection, Her Heart's Gateway

I promise I did not steal the "First Love" concept from Victoria Secunda, the ground-breaking author of several books evaluating family relationships and their effect on a person's development. However, the Father as First Love is one of the main topics in her discussions of the father-daughter relationship.

A quick perusal of some of her most cited quotes makes the impact of this concept clear. "When fathers are lovingly involved with their daughters from birth," she says, "the daughters reap the benefits all their lives. Daughters who had fathers they could count on are the most likely to be drawn to men who treat them well." She adds, "The good father does not have to be *perfect*. Rather, he has to be good *enough* to help his daughter to become a woman who is reasonably self-confident, self-sufficient, and free of crippling self-doubt, and to feel at ease in the company of men."[2] This psychologist's findings go into great depth concerning the positive impact a loving father can have on his daughter's future relationships.

On the other end of the spectrum, however, she points out, "The psychological absence of fathers can be nearly as devastating as a physical absence. When fathers are alive but not a predictable presence actively participating in their daughter's lives, the relationship becomes a permanent 'maybe'."[3] Secunda's book even goes so far as to say, "Father absence has been implicated in anorexia nervosa, in which daughters may exhibit literal father hunger by starving themselves."[4] To be sure, daughters need their fathers not just to be present but to be affectionately present.

I promised you this book would not be a study in psychology, so I will not detail any further psychological research into the female need for affection. I just want to offer you some ideas about how to play the role of First Love in a way that sets your daughter up to have a life of love even after you are gone.

One Day You'll Be Gone ... So Do It Now

I do not mean that in a morbid way. Even if you are not "gone" gone, there will come a time in your relationship with your girl when she must move on. When my girls were old enough not just to date but to seriously consider suitors for marriage, a most curious scripture came to mind: "He must increase; I must decrease."[5] This was John the Baptist's reaction when the people he had been attending to so lovingly began turning their attentions to the new rabbi on the scene, Jesus. Somehow John knew that this was what he had been preparing the people for in the first place. He might have been the first voice they responded to, but he was not supposed to be their whole life's love. He was ready to become less important because he had done his very best when he was most important.

That is how I began to feel when my girls were ready to meet their future husbands. To quote Victoria Secunda one more time,

> If father and daughter can manage to cross the finish line of her emancipation together—she accepting Daddy's flaws, he viewing hers as opportunities for her to learn and grow—the ups and downs of their relationship and mutual

growth can prepare her for the ambiguities of life. The example of the father weathering his own emotional seasons can help the daughter weather her own.[6]

One day, your baby girl will set out to sea without Daddy. How she remembers your affection will either be a wind in her sails or a drag on her progress.

Ok, But How?

If showing affection does not come naturally to you, that is ok. Replacing a blown transformer at the top of a highline pole does not come naturally either, but if you want to be a county lineman, you will learn how to do it. Dismantling and repairing oil field machinery do not come naturally, but if you want to make oil field hand money, you will learn how to do them. Performing a craniotomy does not come naturally, but if you want to be a brain surgeon …

You get the point. Showing affection to your daughter might not come naturally, but you have already been hired as Daddy, so you must learn to do it. We as dads must learn to show affection to our daughters with our touch, our attentions, and our words.

#1. Loving TOUCH

People need to be touched. Too many historical and sociological studies have proven this for me to belabor the point. People need hugs and handshakes, kisses, and pats on the back. People need to sit right next to each other, to lock their arms together, to hold hands. We are touch-driven people.

When COVID-19 first touched the USA and we were on a stay-at-home order for a solid week (the first of so many weeks we stopped counting), I posted to Facebook:

> Louisianians are having hug withdrawals … the whole reason we're a hotspot for Corona-transmission is because we're the huggingest state in America. We hug each other all day long. I hug complete strangers just because they either look like they need it or because they look like their hug will do me good.

Indeed, Sha, daz da trūt.[7] People need to be touched.

PDA—Public Displays of Affection

And it is even more true that your daughter needs a touch from *Dad, her First Love.* A girl registers love levels by whether the one who loves her is willing to touch her in public. Girls must be the reason high schools have PDA rules. When boys want to touch, they do not necessarily want to touch out in the open, but girls insist on holding hands in the hallway where everyone else can see.

Remember this when your girl is young. To hold her daddy's hand in public means everything. To have him hug her tight before she gets on the bus for her field trip is priceless. It tells the whole world that her First Love loves her. A dad's firm hand on his young daughter's knee while they sit in the basketball stands shows the basketball players that she is valuable to someone and she is covered by a strong arm. A kiss from her dad right in front of all her friends opens their eyes to why she is not love-starved for boys like many of them are.

When my Sarah was a high school junior, she interrupted my English class to bring me a message from the front office (she was an office worker). It was one of the first days of school that year, so some of the new students did not know she was my daughter. It turned into one of the most hilarious moments of my teaching career when she bounded up to me and instinctively kissed me right in front of the class. I turned to the class and made a great joke about how we are *really close* at our school. For those who did not know she was my daughter, I wish we had had a camera. This was the ultimate Public Display of Affection.

Holding Hands at Home, etc.

In private, the need for affectionate touch still prevails. Daughters need to hold hands in the car and hug at home. They need Daddy's arm around their shoulder during a movie at home. They need butterfly and Eskimo kisses at bedtime.

My Bethany did not think Eskimos went far enough, so we had to add ear-to-ear, cheek-to-cheek, and chin-to-chin "kisses," too. Each of my girls needed their dad's touch in various measures and at different times. As a little athlete, KaLeigh needed a pat on the butt. As a dreamy romantic, Callie Ruth needed a Ken-Doll daddy to swoop her up in his arms and carry her off into the sunset. Sarah just wanted me to scratch her head. But they all needed the affection of touch. They all loved me to put my hands on the sides of their face or to rest my open palm on the crown of their head. Unless one of us were out of town, I do not think my girls ever went a day without a hug from their dad.

Nevertheless, I have seen dads withhold affectionate touch from their daughters. I am a people watcher; I see the twinges in their countenances and the tightening of their shoulders. I watch for subtle gestures and expressions displaying how they really feel. I have sat brokenhearted as I watched pre-teen girls inch themselves down a bleacher toward their dads, vying for a simple hug, only to be ignored. I have wanted to shake these dads loose from whatever made them so uncomfortable and tell them they are pushing their little girl away.

The Trouble with Touch

I will tell you why it makes a lot of men nervous to show affection to their daughters, especially when it comes to touching. When I did a Scholarly-Google search for "Father-Daughter Affection," the first page of results turned my stomach. Study after study examined the abusive, abnormal relationships between men and their children.

I hate this, but as a pastor, I have counseled grown women who dealt with sexual addictions and self-abuse their whole lives stemming from the abuses they suffered in the quiet night hours at home when their fathers slipped into their bedrooms, and their mothers either slept or wept in the other room. This sort of travesty is devastating, but it must be put in its place as the absurd, sickening, horrifying act that it is. Sadly, the fact that these horrible things have happened in so many families in our society has made today's good fathers paralyzed when it comes to showing their daughters physical affection.

I have seen good dads shy away from holding their daughters in public or having their daughters sit on their laps because they are afraid the Good Touch/Bad Touch police are going to accuse them of perversion. We live in a society where programs like Good Touch/Bad Touch have become necessary, and I am thankful for them, but we cannot allow the abusive behavior of demented men to arrest the beautiful and healthy affection a daddy is supposed to shower on his daughter.

Some of the older generation have experienced these abuses in such silent horror that they are naturally suspicious of others and standoffish with their affections toward children. I have seen the quiet suspicions in their faces when my daughters wanted to cuddle with me in public or when they overheard us mention that our girls sometimes pile up in bed with us to sleep. I determined early on, however, I would not be hindered from showing my daughters the affection they yearn for from *Dad, their First Love*, regardless of what anybody thinks.

The Trouble with *No* Touch

For every woman I have tried to help in the rebuilding of her self-image after having suffered sexual abuse from a father, I have helped multiple others on the opposite end of the suffering—women who never received affection from their daddy. These women deal with emotional deficiencies throughout their lives.

This is where our attention needs to turn as daddies who can learn to do this the right way for our daughters. We need to hear these ladies' stories and determine that we will not leave our daughters out of our affections. One lady in her mid-forties explained to me why she felt so distant from other people and did not think she would ever "have happiness."

The story begins with her father on his death bed. "My dad had leukemia. He had a bone marrow transplant. Then years later, he got lung cancer. I'm not even sure what all he died from. He had a hard life." After offering this brief, cold version of her dad's medical history, she continued, "We never grew up hugging or saying, 'I love you.' But I remember when he was under hospice care. I was there when they said there was nothing more they could do for him. I had to leave the room a minute and the nurse said, 'You okay?' Then Dad said to the nurse about me, 'I wish she would show her emotions or something'."

Here her dad was on his death bed and suddenly he wished his unloved daughter would "show her emotions or something." All this grown daughter could feel was, "Really?"

Imagine the confusion in her heart as the irony of that statement weighed on her. Somehow in his last moments, this dad expected a girl who had never received a hug from him or had never been told "I love you" to gush forth with daughterly affection. It did not happen, and this lady is still searching for what that father never gave her. Many women in our society are searching for what their fathers never gave them.

She Will Be "Loved"

That brings me to a final statement before we finally move on: The dad who withholds affection out of his own insecurities or fears will find his daughter seeking affection from someone else.

She might never get to be loved the way she yearns to be, but she will find someone willing to touch her with the semblances of affection. Whether you like to think about it or not, your daughter needs to find affection through being touched physically. You can either be the one with the hugs, the kisses, and the fatherly caresses, or someone else will arrive to fill her need. I am afraid you cannot be sure of the purity of that person's intentions.

#2. Loving ATTENTIONS

Touch is not the only semblance of affection your daughter is looking for from *Dad, her First Love*. Any positive attention you have to offer will fit the bill. To get a full list or to get inspiration in a moment, ask yourself, *What "attentions" do people give and receive to display their love?*

Your answers will likely boil down to a couple of biggies: time and money, for instance. Do not forget, however, along with your time and money, the objects of your affection—i.e., the ladies in your home—might expect any number of miscellaneous attentions, known in another era as chivalry.

Time

One well-known public speaker often says, "Love is spelled T-I-M-E."[8] Your daughter would agree with this guy. Where and how a man spends his time will tell you where and what he loves. A person's presence says everything about them. I do not mean their aura, either; I mean their location. The idea of being present can make or break a daddy-daughter relationship. "Being there" is the anchoring principle of all parenting.

Some of my best friends are not my best friends because they always have the right answer to my problems or because they know just what to say. Rather, they are my best friends because they are the ones who are present. I do not mind taking long trips with these guys because I do not have to keep a conversation going; I can just sit there and let the time be the teller.

On that note, each one of my girls has gotten to take a separate road trip with just me, where we were able to test this principle (and learn each other's music). These trips were not super expensive; they were just us ... and whatever mission we were on. The time on these trips was priceless because they provided a simple chance for us just to sit in each other's presence.

If your job keeps you away from your girl, that is one thing. If you find other ways to invest in her emotionally, she is smart enough to know that your career just happens to be one of those weird ones where the time is spread out differently. However, when you have a chance to be with her, but you choose your friends, your TV, or your hobbies instead, the wound in her heart will not respond to logical excuses.

Time with each other can be as simple as any daddy-daughter date or half a song's worth of a dance in the kitchen. She just needs time with you. She needs time with you even if it is quiet time. Do not underestimate how important it could be for you just to take a nap together or even just to spend time binging your favorite Netflix series. When she is older, *Parks and Rec* will always make her think of her daddy (yes, you are Ron Swanson ... That is why you need this book).

My youngest daughter and I watch *Bob's Burgers* whenever we get a chance; she even painted me a canvas of Bob and Louise, labeled with our names instead of theirs (I am not making a cartoon recommendation here ... she was an older teen when we started this). My oldest girl and I visit our favorite burger dive. My redhead and I practice jokes on each other in case she makes it to the comedy bar one day. Each of my girls is the kind of friend I was talking about earlier. I enjoy hanging out with them. Call me a fanatic, but my favorite place to be is wherever my wife and girls are. It always has been, and the time I spend with them says to them, "Your First Love loves you too."

Haha. My Callie-Ruth, home from college to figure out what to do with the next phase of her life, just said, "Hey, Dad, I know you need to keep writing, but would you want to watch an episode of *Brooklyn Nine Nine* with me?" Could she have had any better timing? ... I will finish this chapter later.

Money

You can also see where a man's heart is by watching his wallet. Jesus said it this way: "Where your treasure is, there will your heart be also" (Matthew 6:21 KJV).

Believe me, your daughter knows this intuitively as she looks for signs of your affection. She is certainly not a "gold digger" at nine years old; that is not what I am saying. To make this clear, however, here is a story from one lady very dear to me.

With tears in her eyes, this lady in her 70s told me how her father had misplaced his monetary affections throughout her upbringing. Her father was a spendthrift when it came to things *he* wanted. If he needed a new toy or the neighbors were in financial trouble, he proved to be quite a generous soul. However, his own daughter's needs never moved his needle.

One day when she was almost old enough to leave home, she and her dad faced a blowup that had been building up her whole life. Somehow, he sensed a tone of ingratitude in something she said, so he began a tirade about how much money she had cost him her whole life. In that moment, she broke. From her perspective, he had hardly ever spent a dime on her. A place to sleep and food to eat, yes, but she went without everything else she had ever needed—unless she found a way to pay for it. From her preteen years onward, she held odd jobs for her own money.

On the day of this argument, in a final, eye-opening moment for her dad, she toured him through her room: "Find one thing in this room that you ever bought me!" She flung open the closet door where a wardrobe of handmade clothes all hung, sewn by her own hands with fabric she purchased on her own: "Point to one outfit you bought for me, Daddy, just one!" He could not. This dad had never grasped his daughter's pain and rejection in the face of believing her daddy's monetary affections would never be hers.

No one is saying to shower your daughter in gifts, but a thoughtful gift or an extra touch of spending money will tell her you were thinking about her when you stopped at the bank.

Now that we are talking about money, I would be remiss in not mentioning a whole lot of dads who do not have a whole lot of money in the bank. I never had a lot of it when my daughters were young. Honestly, this led to some difficult, dark emotional times for me because I could never "keep up with the Joneses." The Jones's daughters always had better stuff than my daughters and were able to do more things than mine. I never squandered money on my own habits, though, so my daughters never doubted that I would give them a few nice things if I could. And the truth is, we were much better off than many others, and my girls had plenty of nice things.

The point about money is not actually about money. Maybe it is more about thoughtful gifts. They say thoughtful gifts are one of the main five love languages, so in theory, gifts are more important to some girls than others, but every girl appreciates being thought about. Please think about that when you go on a business trip or you and your wife get to have a getaway without the kids; kids still wait at home wondering what little gift their daddy bought for them when he was gone.

Being thought about, being prioritized, being prized … those speak of attention, which your daughter is looking for to feel your affection.

Chivalry

Whether you have a lot of time and money at your disposal or not, there is one more way to make sure your daughter knows she is the object of your affection. It might sound like a throwback to a bygone era, but our generation is due a tiny dose of Chivalry.

Before I go too far, please note I do not ascribe to the notion that women are necessarily the "weaker sex." As you will see in Chapter 6, I am a proponent of equality in male-female relationships of all kinds. I am not your typical southern authoritarian patriarch. However, I believe being a gentleman toward others, especially the women in your home, goes a long way in showing them how much you love them.

I went overboard on a few things in our home, like insisting on opening my wife's and daughters' doors in almost every circumstance. I definitely got my point across to them, but being a stickler about this gentlemanly habit got us all wet on rainy days. I do not propose that dads should open doors for their daughters so much as to handicap them, but it is still a gesture of affection they will appreciate when appropriate.

Gentlemen who stand when a woman enters the room or who walk between her and traffic to keep her from being splashed with street water should not be considered "chauvinists." A gentleman soldier should faithfully follow a female general into battle but still open the door for her on the way to the mess hall. If there is a contradiction in this, at least it is an error on the side of affection. I want the girls in my home to know I value them, including the part of their feminism that remains feminine.

We do not have to call it *chivalry*, but whatever you call it, acts of kindness toward your daughter go a long way in assuring her of your affection. If you drop everything at a moment's notice to run a new set of clothes to her at her drive-through-window job where she has had an embarrassing mishap, she will never forget it. When you get up to refill her water at a regular evening meal, her heart will notice. If you stay up half the night to help her memorize a poem for her class presentation the next day, you will not need to write her any poems yourself. She will know how special she is. And if you drive 14 hours across four states to take her to lunch for her birthday, you will qualify for years of her admiration.

As *Dad, her First Love*, your acts of kindness speak volumes. She reads between the lines very well. After all, she is a girl.

#3. Careful WORDS

Let's close this discussion of loving affections with a few words about our words. Words generate affection more than all the touch and attentions you can give. To be sure, this paragraph could be filled with clichés you have heard all your life about how words start wars and negotiate peace, how they woo the heart of a woman or steel a man's resolve. The self-help and religious literature of the past century are replete with theses on the power of your words.

Earlier we mentioned that ugly words and harsh criticisms have no place in a healthy father-daughter relationship, so now we can focus on the amount of healing, hope, health, and happiness the positive words of your daughter's First Love can bring her.

"I Love You"

We might as well start with the big three: "I LOVE YOU."

I have heard people argue that our generation is wearing this endearment out, but I do not believe it ... and neither does your daughter. Your daughter would never tire of hearing "I love you" from *Dad, her First Love*. I have made it a habit never to leave the house without saying it because I want it to be the last thing my family hears. We say it when we wake up; we say it when we say good night; and we say it like a broken record throughout the day. You could say I say it too much, but my daughters do not think so. They want to hear it. It is almost supernatural, but it is not: it is the natural language of every yearning heart.

While we are talking about these three words, I must point out that they are indeed *three* words, not just two. I might strike you as a hair-splitter on this issue, but please hear me out. "I love you" and "Love you" say entirely different things to a female heart. I do not know how to explain it; it is just true.

I am sure if all you can get out is "Love you," your daughter will still feel special, but when you add your true self to the beginning of it, she feels it. If what I am saying is not true, then why do the two phrases feel so different to you when you say them out loud? When you add "I" to the beginning of it, you are selling yourself out. You are all in with no turning back. You are placing yourself in your daughter's dream of being loved. Instead of just "Love you," give her all three words. Give them to her however you can.

One reason words are so powerful is that they are so versatile. They can be expressed in so many ways. I am not trying to be poetic; I want to take a pragmatic turn and talk about some of the best ways to get our words into our daughter's hearts, to let them know we love them. Like we have already said, you can use your mouth and just say it, but there are other media where words can find their expression and make their way into the eternal recesses of your daughter's memory.

Written Notes

Girls keep shoeboxes full of notes. That should tell us something. A girl prizes every note she ever receives. How precious do you think it would be for her to receive a note from *Dad, her First Love* every now and then to place in her shoebox.

One of the most life-changing moments of my teenage years was when my mom wrote me a confusing note, confusing because it was entirely backward. When I held it up to a mirror, I could read the first line, "I know your life seems a little backward right now … " and then she went on to tell me she was there for me if I needed her, etc. I have never forgotten just that one note from my mom.

Another idea for note-writing I heard only recently from my niece's new husband. Joe told me that every Christmas, each member of his family writes a note for each of the others and places it in their stocking. The note recounts at least one great memory they had together during the past year and then looks forward to one thing they hope to see happen for them in the next. With these once-a-year notes, Joe's family expresses their love for each other in keep-able words.

With all this shoebox talk of keeping notes, I would be surprised to find that all my girls' notes from me turned into keepsakes. I would be surprised because most of them were on their napkins in their lunchboxes. I was the lunch maker for most of my girls' school years, so I got to draw disposable pictures on their brown paper bags and write notes which were about to have Cheeto stains smeared all over them. Even though they threw my notes away, the job of the words had been done. They knew I loved them and had thought enough of them to put it into words.

For you daddies who have newborns, your daughter would love this next idea of written notes. When my first daughter was born, I got gung-ho on how I was going to love this little girl, so I decided to keep a journal for her to chronicle my feelings and her accomplishments every day.

When my second daughter was born the next year, as long as I could keep it up, I kept writing to both of them in their journals every day. Then another year later, my third daughter was born. I tried to stay daily on my journaling commitments, but writing in three journals every night became impossible, so I slowed down a bit. Then two years later, my last one was born, and I was completely worn out.

I still wrote in all their journals, but it was sporadic at best. Even though I fell short from my original goal, the written notes in those journals will be in my girls' shoeboxes for the rest of their lives. I presented each daughter her journal somewhere around her late teens when she was either heading off to college or facing some other growth challenge. To see her surprised by memories of being eight months old slobbering all over daddy or two years old teaching herself to tie her shoes ... hundreds of memories preserved which would have been lost ... The memory of giving her those memories made it worth any trouble it took to write them.

Texts and Social Media Posts

If you do not feel as comfortable writing notes, or maybe your handwriting is just too terrible to read, you are in luck. We live in the 21st century! In today's world of instant messaging and video-capturing of memories, my journal-writing idea is probably outdated anyway. Nevertheless, you can find what works for you.

There is nothing like a deliberate text to show your daughter how much you love her or how proud you are of who she is. When the last words she reads on the way to bed are, "I think you looked really cute in your volleyball outfit, especially when you pancaked that save in the final volley," she will go to bed knowing someone named Daddy noticed the pain she went through for her team, and he thinks a sweaty uniform is pretty. How many thousands of opportunities do you and I have in this electronic age to let our girls know what we think of them! Since we know our words mean so much to our daughters, we should never neglect the potential effect of even one well-worded text.

I am not very consistent in making social media posts, but they go right along with this discussion, and they add the element of PDA mentioned earlier. A social media post where you tag your daughter with a genuine compliment could change her whole world for the day.

I know you might say, "These people get too sappy with this Facebook and Instagram business." You are probably right about that. However, you do not have to be sappy. You do not have to paint a false picture of a rainbow-filled father-daughter relationship. You just need to post a picture occasionally with a caption saying she is yours. If you are not sure how to do it or what to say, get someone to help you. You do not feel bad about letting someone else write those pre-printed poems in your Hallmark cards, so maybe you should not feel bad about getting someone else to come up with your daddy-daughter hashtags. Just the effort you take will make her feel special.

All I know is that posting to social media is the language of your daughter's generation, so it would be nice for her to see some of your words of affection there.

Regular Verbal Compliments

This is all about words of affection. "You are beautiful" has to come from Daddy's mouth! Maybe those are not the exact words you would choose, but come up with as many versions of how to say it as you can. Then say it. Verbal compliments are important to us all.

My daughters are gorgeous. Every one of them takes after their mom in some way, and she is striking. But no matter how beautiful or handsome someone is, they never really believe it unless someone who loves them believes it first … and tells them. We certainly do not want to turn our daughters into narcissists who can't make it through an hour without hearing a new wonderful thing about themselves, but I am willing to bet that is not a problem your daughter will face just because you offer her sincere compliments.

Sometimes, when my daughters doubted their looks or body type, I had to remind them that I was once a young, red-blooded American boy who knew a nice figure when I saw it, so I know what I am talking about when I say all of your body parts are in the right places and are shaped the way they're supposed to be shaped! If your girl lives on the same planet as mine, she needs her daddy to reassure her. Social "norms" can be cruel to a girl's self-image.

I had to say all that about physical beauty because this world does drive our daughters to question their looks. However, compliments from *Dad, her First Love* do not have to be all about lashes and lipstick. Your daughter has innumerable qualities that make her wonderful. Her mind, her humor, her thoughtfulness, her athleticism, her art, her music, her cookies, her ideas, her values, her arguments, her ability to get ready so quickly after sleeping too late … for crying out loud, you have a boundless list of potential things to compliment and praise in your daughter's life.

Pay just enough attention, and you will be able to tell her something you admire about what she has recently said or done. "Good job" is a great start, but if you can say her slide into third base followed textbook precision and is the only reason she wasn't thrown out by the first-base lady's amazing arm, your compliment will register as specific and authentic.

Moreover, you might not know the difference between Bach and Beethoven, but if you can say your daughter's piano recital sounded better than both of them, she will at least know you listened with your special daddy ears. Compliments and praise do not have to be so outlandish; they just need to tell your daughter that her First Love sees her and thinks she is doing fine.

DeAnza Duron, creator of the popular children's video series *The Best Buddies,* summed this whole concept up in a song my girls fell in love with when they were little: "My Daddy's Crazy Nuts (Over Me)." You should look up *The Best Buddies* series for your family. It teaches some of the greatest "getting along" messages your kids could ever learn, all with original music that appeals to the essence of a kid's heart. Just a sampling of the song titles should show you what I mean: "Allergic to Griping," "It's Not Fun If It's Not Fun for Everybody," "Everybody's Taking a Nap," "Sure, I'd Love To."

These titles were all Opbroek family favorites, but the lyrics to "My Daddy's Crazy Nuts (Over Me)" reveal how every little kid yearns for his or her dad's acceptance and approval. Singing about their dad, the kids glow with each line: "He thinks I'm pretty ... funny ... smart as I can be. My daddy's crazy crazy nuts ... over ME." I wish you knew the tune so this would ring in your head like it is in mine right now, but let the theme soak in as we move on.[9]

Your daughter values your opinion as highly as anyone else's in her whole world. She could be down to her very last ounce of energy and ready to throw in the towel, but if her dad is still smiling from her corner, she will fight another round. Her friends will come and go. Her teachers will inspire her only for a season. Her fans will be fickle like all fans are. But her daddy will always be her daddy, and she will remember his opinion, his words, his gestures, and facial expressions for the rest of her life. Whether or not you knew what you were getting into, you will always be her first love, and your words will always matter to her.

Love Others When She's Watching

Your time, attentions, and words mark an accurate level for her to check the depth of your affection, but her observations do not stop with how you treat only her. Looking back at the opening of this chapter, you will remember the concept of walking in love as a lifestyle.

A Lifestyle of Love

When a man has a lifestyle of love, his family reaps the benefits. The way her daddy treats others becomes the classroom where a girl learns how to love. Again, this is one of those concepts which remain as steady as the laws of physics. You and I do not get to opt out of these natural laws. Even if you do not agree with gravity, for instance, it will still make your trip to the ground from the top of a ladder painful, and whether or not you believe it, your daughter is affected by watching how you treat others.

"Love your neighbor as you love yourself" is as basic to our psyche as bringing food to our mouths is basic to our physique. Every person knows intuitively that we must eat food to survive, and none of us resists the urge. Ironically, the urge to treat others the way we want to be treated is just as intuitive, yet we do not do it.

Well, I say we do not; maybe you do. If you do, great job! You are well on your way to showing your daughter what real love is. This goes for every relationship from how you talk about your boss to how you react to the cashier at the grocery store and how you treat your spouse ... especially how you treat your spouse.

Love Her Mom[10]

I have discovered the million-dollar secret about the daddy-daughter love connection. This one might sting, but it is true. Your daughter values how you love your spouse even more than she values your love for herself. I want to pause so that sentence can sink in. I did not mistype it.

I have sat with husbands and wives who waited until their daughters were in their twenties before they decided to go through a long-time-coming divorce. They stayed together for years because they wanted their kids to have stability at home, but now, after their daughter is out in the world trying to find a family of her own, suddenly she is blindsided to find out her observations at home were bogus. You are young enough reading this book to curtail this. You can find a way to love your spouse. The world is full of books, videos, seminars, and personal coaches who can help you get your spousal love on.

I remember watching my dad chase my mom around the house, popping her on the behind, and acting like he would prefer to be in the back room with her than in the living room with us. When I was 10, I acted like that was gross, but it registered with me as something couples should feel between each other. My daughters are the same. "Oooo, gross, Daddy" actually means, "I am so happy! My daddy loves my mommy! Yay!"

Openness about your affection toward your spouse is more fun than pretending to be prudish, anyway. I have never understood families who avoid talking about "sex and stuff" when they know good and well "sex and stuff" is on everyone's mind! Your daughter might giggle and turn red, but the truth is she loves it when you chase your wife, joke about making out, or act like you are really looking forward to getting your wife alone. She sees it like she sees a movie.

Remember, though, movies do not go from reel to reel with only happy love scenes. They also take us through the characters' conflicts and misunderstandings, and as much as it might scare your daughter to hear the conflicts or mis-understandings between you and your wife, love can be displayed in the worst of times too. When there is trouble brewing, it might thrill her all the more to see you in love and resolving conflict with love. Let your love for your wife show. Be passionate when you can. Treat her with all the affection mentioned in this chapter. How you treat her matters to your daughter.

As I alluded to earlier, being affectionate with your wife in front of your daughter is even more important than being affectionate with your daughter herself. A dance in the kitchen with your daughter is special, as we have already noted, but a dance in the kitchen with your wife tells your daughter that there might be someone like you for her who will one day love her the way you love her mommy.

Closing Thought: You Are the "Authority" on Love

If you do all the things in this chapter well, but she does not see the same feelings between you and your wife, her heart will know something is not right. You see? You will always be *Dad, her FIRST Love*, but you will not always be her only love. Early on, she will begin to yearn for a mate, and you are showing her now how a husband chooses his wife over everything and everyone else. You are showing your daughter how she should be treated when she finds her *second* love.

Choose your wife! Defend your wife! Side with your wife! Become one heart with your wife! Drill these admonitions into your own head until they are a part of your innermost being, and your daughter will grow up with a fundamental understanding of how she wants to be loved.

As *Dad, her First Love,* you are the one with the authority to teach her about love. She cherishes your authority in the matter and needs your authority in her life, which leads us to the next stage of your Daddy responsibilities as you work out the details of fatherhood.

You have the authority to teach her discipline. She is enrolled in your academy and ready to toe the line for you while you wear your next hat, *Dad the Dean of Discipline.*

[1] 1 Corinthians 13

[2] "Victoria Secunda Quotes (Author of *When You and Your Mother Can't Be Friends*)." Goodreads. www.goodreads.com/author/quotes/48987.Victoria_Secunda.

[3] Ibid.

[4] Ibid.

[5] John 3:30, *Berean Study Bible*

[6] "Victoria Secunda Quotes (Author of *When You and Your Mother Can't Be Friends*)." Goodreads. www.goodreads.com/author/quotes/48987.Victoria_Secunda.

[7] Indeed, baby, that's the truth.

[8] Fred Lowery Ministries. https://fredlowery.com/

[9] https://thebestbuddiesmusic.com/

[10] I have a traditional family, but if you are not married to your daughter's biological mom, just rename this section to include your significant other. If you are divorced from her mom, you can still do your best to show love to her mom in an honoring, caring way.

5

Dad the Dean of Discipline

I grew up believing my dad was a drill sergeant. Now that I am old, I know better. He is a softy, genuinely kind and considerate. However, with me and my two brothers, he got his bluff in early. His military flat-top, martinet bark, and commanding presence told us he was not one to be crossed, and—believe you me—mutiny never crossed our minds. My dad's gruff expressions and threats—e.g., he would "give us something to cry about;" we would be punished double at home if we ever got in trouble at school, etc.—were enough to make us walk a straight line.

Get That Bluff In Early

Truth be told, my brothers and I stayed out of trouble, by and large, because we had a healthy fear of a man who would never hurt a soul. In his honor, I thought I would call this chapter, "Dad the Drill Sergeant," but I would not want anyone to skip this paragraph and miss the point. You do not have to be a drill sergeant for your kids to revere you and keep the rules of your home. You might, indeed, need to get your bluff in early, and if you do, most of your concerns will be dealt with before they start.

Discipline is not always a bluff, however. If it were, this would be so simple, but since it is not, you might want to put pen to paper and come up with a plan that works for you. The safety and order of your home is an integral part of your daughter's happiness and self-fulfillment. She needs to live within defined borders. The borders can be as flexible as you as the parent choose, but she needs even the flexibility to be defined by you. Your daughter has an innate sense that if she can break through the border herself, then the border is weak, and therefore, she is not safe.

In that sort of environment, she will be compelled to tap into her own little fight-or-flight/survival-of-the-fittest nature in order to feel protected. That is not her job; it is yours. And the smoke and mirrors of your tough demeanor will only last until an actual border violation tests it. That is when you will need the wisdom and determination to be *Dad the Dean of Discipline.*

When it comes to the touchy subject of discipline in the home, there are no experts. There might be theoretical experts out there, but they are not the ones raising your daughter day-in and day-out. Theory does not have to answer for its own mistakes; it leaves the consequences piled up on you, the theory applicator.

Theory's consistency sounds good on paper, but it can make you neglect the needs of your daughter, which might not be consistent moment by moment. My hope for this chapter is that it will encourage you to find what works for your household. I would be glad to know the stories of my trials and errors were not wasted but rather aided you in finding consistency.

Trial & Error

I hate that something as important as discipline would ever become a matter of trial and error, but for various reasons, this remains the case.

First, every child has his or her own personality type. If you have ever been interested in personality studies, then you know there are multiple ways to measure someone's core tendencies, from the Myers-Briggs Type Indicator to the Enneagram numbering system, which is all the rave right now. Nowadays, there are dozens of ways to define a personality type, and to administer discipline perfectly for each of your children, you would need a personality test completed for each one before they emerge from the womb. Even then, though, your disciplinary actions would be implemented from your own personality type, so every new circumstance would still be laden with mistakes based on how you missed the needs of each child's "true self" because you were operating out of your own "true self."

Then, after you realize every child has his or her own personality type, you also have to come to terms with the other factors vying for their role on this stage; family structure, geographical placement, cultural surroundings, and even economic indicators will all have a say in your decisions as *Dad the Dean of Discipline*.

No set of all-encompassing instructions will ensure the proper dispensing of discipline in your home. Honestly, even if you could memorize a playbook on disciplinary decision-making, you would soon run into trouble when you discover you are playing on an ever-changing field. As your daughter ages, as she experiences life-events that you cannot control, as world events shift around you, your playbook will become outdated by the day.

How Do You Know It's Working?

All of this and more should tell us that our success as the *Dean of Discipline* cannot be measured by checklists on disciplinary clipboards. Instead, our success must be measured by the observable intangibles we pray our children acquire. Those intangibles have made their way into "Books of Virtue" for thousands of years of human history and instruction. What we are hoping to develop in our daughters is kindness, goodness, faithfulness, stewardship, teachability, wholesomeness, appropriateness, honesty, fairness, etc.

The list is endless. These are the virtues by which we judge our methods. When we see these qualities in our daughters, we know whatever method of discipline we have chosen must be working. If these are lacking, then so are we.

Trial & Error it is, then, and that leads to the structure of this chapter. Knowing that to offer you techniques which worked for me would only help you if you happen to be raising girls who are just like mine, I thought, instead, I could share with you a few principles I found helpful. These principles guided me through the roughest times of parenting.

You might remember from when we talked about boys a couple of chapters ago, sometimes your daughter needs you to be the "bad guy," but when it comes to discipline, it often feels like you are the perpetual "bad guy." No one likes that (unless you have a Clint Eastwood complex and really want these punks to make your day every day). Because I do not like being the bad guy, I fell back on some principles that protected me and allowed me to be who I wanted to be while having to play the role of *Dad the Dean of Discipline*.

Three Guiding Principles

Guiding Principle Number One: Don't Frustrate Her

This first principle, "Don't Frustrate Her," was born from part of a scripture that simply says, "Fathers, don't exasperate your children" (Ephesians 6:4a NIV). In a more archaic version of the same scripture, you could read, "And, ye fathers, provoke not your children to wrath" (KJV). Whichever way you think says it better, the principle is the same: "Dad, do not frustrate your daughter; she has enough to deal with without you driving her to become exasperated and angry."

This scripture encouraged me to be vigilant concerning my own actions ... maybe even as much as I was concerned with my daughters'. If I found myself pushing her buttons, so to speak, I was most likely adding even more befuddlement to a bad situation. Even if her behavior still needed to be corrected in one way or another, there were certain mistakes I could avoid if I wanted to be faithful to this principle of parenting. Therefore, I compiled a mental list to avoid. I am not sure I did a good job avoiding them all, but at least I was aware of my own error so I could apologize if necessary. Here is the list of frustrating errors we dads should try to avoid.

Frustrating Errors to Avoid

Yelling

I am apparently a yeller. I think of myself as mild-mannered, but I have been asked by my family on more than one occasion, "Do you realize you're yelling?" Please catch the understatement in "more than one occasion." The fact is I am very guilty of yelling and have deceived myself into believing otherwise.

In my defense, I do have a job where voice projection is a plus, but one day I listened to a recording of myself and could not believe how angry I sounded when I thought I was calm. Ever since hearing that CD, I have tried not to yell. Moreover, I have finally realized there is no call for a raised voice when my daughters (or wife) are only three feet away.

I had to admire one person I met who claimed never to have raised their voice at their family. Hearing their story of peaceful conflict resolution convicted my conscience, but then afterward I thought it over and figured they must be lying … or they must be the most boring person on earth.

Kidding aside, I do try not to yell. Yelling at your daughter is wrong. Of course, she can suck it up and forgive you later, but please do not act as if it is not something to be forgiven. It is. When we scream and holler, turning red in the face, we are most likely evidencing the fact that we do not have our stuff together any better than our kids do. At the very least, we should think of speaking in a calm tone just to hide our own hypocrisy. That way no one will realize you are actually frustrated with yourself, and no one will have to shag your fouls as you sling words off in every possible direction.

How flustered do you need your daughter to be in order to get your point across, anyway? Do you need her heart pattering, knees knocking, and lip quivering at the booming voice blasting her for something she has done? The frustration itself has probably blocked off her short-term memory so she does not even remember why you started yelling.

No one is condemning the undulation of voice that certain conversations require. Disagreements and moments of correction will often fill the atmosphere with swaying emotion and essential animation. However, if you want to refrain from frustrating her, you will not try to win a match through the intimidation of your loud voice. Look back at yourself from her perspective and listen to yourself with her ears. Her perception of your voice is what matters, and yelling frustrates her.

Violent Outbursts

Perception plays an important role in all the disciplining scenarios of your household. What one person feels is an innocent tantrum, another might view as a demonstration of a violent temper. There comes a point in a dad's life when he has to decide how he wants to be perceived.

I joked a little about raising our voices too much, but intimidating, violent behavior is no joke at all. Violence is an absolute violation of any principle regarding how we discipline our daughters (or your sons for that matter). Throwing things, pushing people, squeezing their frail arms, shaking them, scaring them, striking them with violent force … these are not just calls for frustration; they are calls for intervention.

I had to mention it here as a part of this principle, but if you have to fight urges of violence that could lead to harming anyone or even damaging property, please consider reaching out to someone for help. I know "counseling" can sound extreme, but it might surprise you to find that a professional counselor can offer you simple solutions to your outbursts of violence. Violence goes beyond "frustrating." Your daughter deserves a violence-free home, the "safe-haven" we committed to as *Dad, Security Detail.*

Belittling and Sarcastic Language

I feel like I have taken a downer as I trudge through these areas where so many of us have frustrated our children and spouses, but I hope the somber tone of this section will play out as a steady reminder that our actions and words matter. When we bring correction to our daughters, certain modes of operation should remain off-limits. Another one of those modes is the act of belittling, even with playful sarcasm.

I try not to, but I have a strange tendency to belittle my family when they take a little longer to figure something out than I figure they should have taken. I am a little ashamed to admit it, but it is not like I just deliberately set out to talk them down.

What happens is that I will struggle with a problem … let's say, for instance, how to fit all the luggage into the trunk of the car on the first leg of a long trip. It might take me 15 minutes of alternating the Tetris pieces to organize it all perfectly. However, the next day when we load back up from the first hotel stay, if someone else is looking at the same problem, I make them feel stupid for not immediately seeing where everything should go. That might be a terrible example, but it is a terrible habit, so we can leave it at that. The point is that it will frustrate your daughter if you belittle her.

Word to the wise, also, when it comes to sarcasm, your daughter is most likely still at a literal developmental level with her language processing skills, so even if you think you are being funny, she thinks you are serious. On top of that, even if you try to explain your sarcasm, the explanation will go over her head. When she is lying in her bed trying to fall asleep, she will still be processing the literal meaning of whatever you said.

I do not think there is an exact age when the brain begins processing sarcasm as the humorous figurative language it is supposed to be; each brain is on its own timer. Remember this when your 10-year-old hasn't completed her chores and you remark, "I suppose you can sweep the kitchen whenever you get around to it; these Cheerios won't hurt anything once they're ground into the grout." If she still has not swept within the next few hours, you need to consider that her brain thinks you gave her permission to put it off. If you yell at her later, her sense of justice will tell her that you are the one in the wrong.

Some adults do not even get sarcasm, so if you plan to keep it in your vocabulary, try to tag a direct explanation onto the end of it. Your daughter will appreciate the directness, and she might learn a little earlier how to interpret figurative language.

We are talking about how to avoid bringing our daughters to a point of frustration. There is nothing wrong with well-played sarcasm. I have a whole list of Shakespearean insults from my teaching years if you need them. You can use them to degrade your buddies over politics, sports, or their hygiene habits. If, for instance, one of your friends neglects to shower, feel free to call him "the rankest compound of villainous smell that ever offended nostril."[1] Also, you can greet your beer-bellied buddy with "Peace, ye fat guts!"[2] End your next political debate with "More of your conversation would infect my brain"[3] or "Methink'st thou art a general offense and every man should beat thee."[4]

But when your daughter comes downstairs with no make-up on, do not say, "I am sick when I do look on thee."[5,6] That would not sit well with her. I dare say it will frustrate her a little.

Public Shaming

It is one thing to slip up at home with a little sarcasm or a tone which is a bit rough, but please heed this next warning as if I were telling you your hair is on fire. Your daughter does not need to be shamed publicly.

A wave of public shaming incidents on social media platforms a few years ago made me fear for some fathers who might have destroyed their daughters' trust indefinitely. As *Dad the Dean of Discipline*, it is true you will need to create consequences for broken rules, but publicly shaming your daughter makes you better suited to wear the hat of villain, as if you were living out a 17th-century puritan novel where you have forced the adulteress to wear an "A" on her chest.

I have found myself biting my tongue in public, holding my peace until we were away from her friends, and allowing myself to look like the loser of the moment, all to avoid the possibility of shaming a daughter in public. Even when my daughters were only four or five years old attempting a coup in the grocery store, I would lean down to one of their ears and with a cordial smile let her know, "You look like you're winning now because I will not embarrass you in public, but we will be at the van soon, and you might want to rethink your behavior before we get there."

I feel that strongly about this principle, and I hope I can encourage you to make public shaming taboo too. The memory of public shaming lasts a lifetime. If you embarrass your daughter on purpose, she will turn 82 years old one day, still rehearsing that moment with dread. Please avoid it.

Religious Rebukes

For those of you in religious homes, mark well another error that could set your daughter on a negative course for the rest of her life.

When I was a teenager, I remember sitting at my friend's dining room table when he said something that could have been considered "sinful." His mom's reaction sounded pious, but it struck me as dangerous, and indeed turned out to be a turnoff for her son's future spiritual journey. Aghast at what she had heard, and possibly overreacting because they had a guest at the table (me), she asked her son, "What would Pastor Jones[7] think if he heard you say that?" As I have thought back over her rebuke, especially now that I am a pastor myself, I have often said, "No wonder kids aren't excited about going to church. Their parents tell them the pastor is the sin-inspecting Gestapo."

I have seen the same phenomenon—only on a much larger scale and with more devastating consequences—when parents use the Bible as a "paddle" for disciplining their children. I'm not trying to play Pollyanna here, but if a child's main interaction with Scripture is to hear it point out her errors and make her feel like a reprobate, her parent is defeating the purpose of the Bible.

I know this next example sounds extreme, but I was called to one family's home because the daughter apparently needed a demon exercised. When I arrived, the girl was writhing on the sofa in your typical Stephen-King style, making the whole atmosphere eerie. The parent explained to me that this daughter had been disobedient and now needed a demon cast out of her, but this time they needed a pastor's power.

I asked the girl to stop writhing and sit up so I could ask a few questions. She did. After discovering that this family had always equated childhood disobedience with demonic-level habitation, I explained to them that they did not have a demon problem; they had a theology problem. We talked for a couple of hours about our shared human frailties, our common need for forgiveness, and the struggles we all face as people ... without any need for demonic aid in our own foolishness.[8] The atmosphere in the room lightened as this girl's countenance registered a fresh understanding of God's grace. To my knowledge, this precious young lady never displayed her "demonic" behavior again.

That episode might be an outlier, but please heed the spirit of what I am saying: If you use your Bible, your church, or your pastor as a tool of punishment, the results might not be what you hoped for. No matter what your religion is, if your kid thinks she will suffer eternal torment for not cleaning her room, her feelings toward your church might not be as cozy as you wish they would be. Don't we want the elements of our faith to be a source of peace and comfort to our children? Don't we want the trials and failures of their futures to drive them home and not farther away?

Sitting at the table with my friend and his family so many years ago, I determined that one day when I had kids of my own, I would not allow them to see the pastor or the church as their enemy. I want their expectations for religion to be higher than that.

Lack of Clarity in Expectations

I wish I could write a whole chapter about the next way we parents often frustrate our children. I have spoken at length on the subject when teaching kids how to make themselves trustworthy so their parents will offer them greater freedoms. The subject revolves around expectations.

In these talks with teens, I try to encourage them to pin their parents down for specific expectations they can meet to prove they are growing in trustworthiness. The idea is simple. Dad might be telling you to "do your best" in school and Mom might be telling you to "be modest and ladylike" with your boyfriend, but you need to pin Mom and Dad down to tell you exactly what they mean. Ask your dad, "What grade are you looking for me to make, Dad? When you tell me to do my best, it feels like you are expecting me to get straight A's, but what grade will you be ok with in my killer chemistry class?" For Mom, the daughter gets to ask, "Mom, you keep telling me to be modest and keep my purity, but what are you really expecting? Is there a certain type of kissing and touching you're telling me not to do? Can I kiss my boyfriend at all, or do you mean for us just to hold hands?"

I wish you could see the lights come on for these adolescents when they realize the reason their parents always seem disappointed is that no one in the home has ever clarified their expectations.

There is a strange and deranged psychology at play when we hold secret expectations for people. It is almost as if we want to be disappointed. We must have some sort of complex that makes us like being resentful when other people let us down. Then again, there is always that chance your relationship with someone is so magical that they will meet your secret expectations without ever being told what you expect. Wouldn't that be something!

Well, regardless of what pathology leads people to keep expectations hidden, the results are frustrating, to say the least. If you have ever been on the side of a relationship where you could never figure out what to do to make the other person happy, then it should not be difficult for you to imagine your daughter's frustration when she does not know exactly what you expect from her. If she feels like Dad is perpetually disappointed in her, but she cannot figure out why, there must be a lack of clarity between what Dad is *expecting* and what Dad is *saying*.

This applies to everything about your relationship, from how clean you expect her to keep her bathroom to the amount of homework you want to know she has completed. You can think of hundreds of further examples from around your own home. I can tell you for sure, though, your daughter will go from frustrated to flying steady if you clarify specific expectations for her.

It might sound like too much work to think of specific expectations for all these aspects of your daughter's behavior, but just try it. Maybe just try it for one month. At the end of a month, measure the atmosphere of your home against what it used to be when both you and your daughter were frustrated because neither of you had clarity on your actual expectations. I believe you will find the results well worth the cost. The peace of mind you both experience might make you expect it all the time. Don't go too far and try to turn her into a programmable robot, but do give her the dignity of offering her precise expectations.

Passive Aggression

Grunting, Pouting, Huffing and Puffing, or Going Silent: these are just a few of the daughter-crushing parenting strategies we will finalize this section with under the topic Passive Aggression.

Passive aggression is unhealthy in any relationship, especially a father-daughter one where direct communication is valued so highly. Passive aggression manifests itself when Dad's feelings have been hurt or he is so frustrated he cannot think of a pragmatic solution to the discipline issue he perceives his daughter is so guilty of.

If you find yourself casting disdain on your daughter's ideas or nitpicking her behavior in areas unrelated to the actual conflict that needs to be resolved head-on, you are operating out of passive aggression. As we will discover when we get into the good ideas of how to bring discipline into our daughter's lives, there are plenty of options besides passively expressing discontent.

I cannot close this discussion without divulging the worst of my passive-aggressive mistakes, the one which will live in Opbroek parenting infamy.

As I mentioned earlier, I have made it a rule never to ignore a call from one of my daughters. Even if I answer them just quick enough to find out whether it is an emergency, I do not let it go to voicemail. This has become such an understood habit that my girls assume if Daddy did not answer his phone, it must have fallen into the toilet or something. Even in the middle of a public speaking engagement, I have answered a daughter's call, hoping secretly to demonstrate a side-point about fatherly love to the audience. After a brief pause and a moment of hushed laughter, I could hear the ladies in the crowd: "Ah, isn't Brian the sweetest dad ever? He never ignores his daughters' phone calls."

Well, one day at home, my youngest daughter and I had a heated disagreement, where she took an authoritative tone I deemed to be entirely out of line. Instead of carrying the conversation any further or even offering a truce until later, I just grabbed my keys and drove away. It was the equivalent of hanging up on someone, but that was only the beginning.

My daughter did not want our talk to end this way, so she immediately dialed my phone to make me talk it out (By this time, as you might have noted, I also violated another personal Daddy rule by not announcing "I love you" when I left the house). Well, instead of answering her call, I pressed the ignore button ... She called again ... I ignored it again ... The next time my phone rang, it was my wife.

She had no idea what had happened to make me so angry, but she was sitting in my living room with a shattered young lady who had never imagined what it would feel like for her daddy to ignore her call. My brilliant, beautiful, solid-core Sarah was in a legitimate panic attack.

In all these years of parenting, I had never once done something so foolish and emotionally harmful. Suddenly, passive aggression had taken a simple issue and turned it into a crushing memory that can never be taken back. Sarah became the first one in my family to experience the rejection of a dad who was angry enough to ignore her. She will always be the last.

Guiding Principle Number Two: The Motivation Check

Obviously, my own pride led to the horrible incident detailed above. My pride had been wounded, and I wanted to show my daughter I had more authority in my little finger (which I used to ignore her call) than I would ever allow her to wield over me. Come hell or high water, I was going to be the man of my house. No one was going to use that tone of voice with me and get away with it.

These feelings are the type of motivation that leads to the *frustrating* parenting errors we just listed above. It stands to reason then, that if we can identify good motivating factors, we will find ourselves implementing better strategies as *Dad the Dean of Discipline*.

When we make parenting decisions of any kind, our first question should be "What is my motivation?" I am afraid ignoring this interrogation of our motives will almost always lead to missing the mark when it comes to useful discipline. Any good Discipline Dean would identify *why* he is enforcing his own rules and regulations. Of course, you do not need to dissect every guideline and explain to your daughter each rule's value for her betterment as a person, but you do need to verify in your own conscience that the betterment of her person is your actual goal. Motivation is a skeleton key to unlock the secrets of our decisions as dads.

Is My Pride on the Line?

I have found several motivations to be counterproductive to fruitful discipline. For instance, as we have already hinted, my motivation for disbursing discipline cannot be because my pride is on the line. If we are at a public event, perchance, and I need all these strangers to know I am in control of my daughter's behavior, I might need to check my motivation before I make any quick disciplinary decisions. Is her behavior embarrassing me in front of my guests? Now would be a good time to process a plan rather than calling down fire for everyone to see. Am I holding the reins so tightly on my girls because I am afraid of what my in-laws or the other members of my extended family might think? Or how about the opinions floating around the country club or church?

When these are my worries, then saving face could trump my better judgment and leave me with a wounded daughter. Understandably, times do arise when the lessons we teach our daughters are aimed at helping us save face. However, if we check the gauges in our heart and find the ego level running over, we might need to reconsider our motivation before implementing any measures of discipline.

Do I Want to Be Liked?

Another question dads have to answer to root out any counterproductive measures of motivation is, "Am I looking to be her friend, or am I willing to be her dad?" To be fair, a friendship between parents and children is beautiful and can be very healthy as we have talked about earlier in this book. I am not disparaging any of our desires to be friends with our daughters. A good dad can be friend and disciplinarian at the same time.

The problem comes when Dad wants to be "liked" more than he wants his daughter to have the character that will make her likable to others. If we avoid confronting some of the real disciplinary issues, like how she speaks to authority figures, how she prioritizes her schoolwork and chores, or how her attitude affects the neighbors, we will be hampering her potential in all of her other relationships.

Whose Benefit Does It Serve?

Her other relationships bring us to another question dads need to ask themselves when approaching the task of discipline: Who benefits from the discipline? We are quick to claim we are punishing her "for her own good," so it would not hurt if we have actually visited the question before we doled out the punishment.

Considering the answer to this question will help you as *Dad the Dean of Discipline* to explain yourself, stay the course, and be sure some sort of character development has occurred in your daughter.

I have often stopped my daughter in the middle of bad behavior to tell her, "There is no way I am going to let you stay this way ... Your future husband will kill me!"

In moments like these, dad and daughter both gain a long-range vision for the discipline of the moment. The same motivation can apply to what sort of student she will be for her future professors, what sort of boss she will be for her future employees, and what sort of mom she will be for her own future children. When you really answer who the discipline is going to benefit, it adds meaning to the consequences of less-than-preferable behavior.

If we consider the lifelong benefits of implementing discipline, it might change how we approach the whole subject. Maybe with this mindset, we can set up goals and objectives just like we would for any plan of success. Maybe we should list the qualities our daughter will find most beneficial to her future and work our game-plan around that list. If honesty, integrity, responsibility, self-regulation, and empathy are the broad strokes you would like your daughter to embody when she is a grown woman, then mark them down and build your plans around them.

Your list might be different from that one, but if you know what your list is—and it would sure be nice for your daughter to agree with your list—then you and your daughter could get on the same page together with some of the discipline needed for the tasks. Suddenly, discipline begins to take on new meaning, less like punishment and more like a lifestyle that produces great results. Instead of frustrating our daughters, we will have established legitimate motivation and empowered our daughters with successful character.

Guiding Principle Number Three: Find A "Rod" That Works (And Use It)

"Spare the rod, spoil the child" conjures varied emotions in our society. For those who believe this aphorism advocates corporal punishment with a bamboo stick, a feeling of protective anger rises within them. As stated earlier, I agree we must protect children from physical abuse. We must be careful, however, not to abandon the lasting truth expressed in this figurative one-liner.

If we abandon all rods of discipline because we believe a child's self-expression (sometimes code word for bad behavior) should never be curtailed, we will wind up with a generation of grown-ups who never consider the feelings and lives of others ahead of themselves. Oops ... we are edging dangerously close to that right now in this generation, so if you feel that any corrective action is paramount to child abuse, please skip to the next chapter. You do not want to read the following suggestions for spoilage-reducing "rods."

Not all of these rods of discipline will work for your daughter. Again, this chapter began by explaining the "trial & error" method of discovering what is best for each of our kids. Honestly, if you can do your best to avoid the missteps of "Principle One: Don't Frustrate Her," you will already be leagues ahead of a lot of other dads spinning their wheels in frustration.

I cannot say I mastered any of the "rods" in the list below, but I tried. I wanted to offer my girls the best chance possible to reach their fullest potential, so as their *Dean of Discipline*, I kept a few rods handy. These are just a few ideas I ran across and/or implemented through the years.

Spanking (Jeepers, that word just sounds terrible now.)

Alright, let's just start with the worst one. When I started as a young father, the only idea I had for keeping my kids in line was a pop on the diaper. A quick swat seemed to let them know that whatever they had done led to pain instead of pleasure.

I know I made some of my extended family mad on at least one occasion. When my oldest girl was not even a year old, rolling through the house in her little walker, she grew very curious about the propane space heater in the living room. It was the middle of summer, so she was in no danger of burning herself, but I popped her little hand anyway. One of the older ladies gasped as if I had committed a crime, but all I could think is that my daughter needs to know the space heater can hurt her if she touches it. If it had been winter, she might have learned the lesson on her own, but we would have had a couple of sleepless nights dealing with burned fingers.

For instances like these, when an alarming pat can imitate the hurtful consequences of real life, I do not regret spanking my girls. As for the later spankings, which could have been replaced with better modes of discipline, I still have not decided whether my conscience is calling for regret. So far, my girls have not sent me any bills for their therapists, so I might be okay. As they grow older, they say they are happy I loved them enough to correct them. When they were between 8 and 11, however, I am sure it did not feel so much like love … unless love is supposed to sting.

I hope the song "Daddy's Hands" will be what they remember when they think of those moments in years to come. However, when they raise their own children, I think they will be well-equipped with other "rods," so they might be able to avoid giving spankings altogether. One of my dear friends, retired Air Force Colonel and professional family counselor, Dr. Bruce Ewing, believes corporal punishment should not even qualify as a rod of last resort. Admittedly, when he was a young father, he also employed spanking, but after years of experience with other effective "rods" of discipline, he advocates for spank-free homes. Your daughter might like for you to take his advice.

Reciprocal Consequences

Operating from a mindset of what I call reciprocal consequences also helped me as *Dad the Dean of Discipline*. Another way to look at this tactic of correction is to choose a "punishment that fits the crime."

Here is a fair and effective example our girls will never forget. Our household chores were rotated on a weekly basis so each girl could share responsibilities and gain equal experience. One of their most important duties was to feed the dog. The consequence of neglecting this duty had to match the relative value of food and water to another living creature who is dependent upon us for survival, so anyone who forgot to refill Buddy's food and water would only eat bread and water for dinner. Yes, sitting at the table with all the rest of us enjoying our food, she would only eat bread and water. It only had to happen a couple of times because they learned quick to take care of their dog.

When your daughter is faced with a reciprocal consequence, her innate sense of justice will be satisfied. Implementing a punishment that matches the crime speaks of fairness.

It is also unique to the behavior, so instead of just being "grounded" all the time, your daughter will be grounded from something specifically related to the wrong choice she made. If she neglects to wash the dishes, she gets an extra week of dish duty. If the ice cream melts because she did not put the groceries away when she was supposed to, then she does not get even a spoonful of ice cream from the next new carton unless she uses her own money to replace this one. If she makes everyone late to an event, then she is required to wake up 10 minutes early and get the morning coffee ready for a solid week.

These all sound like innocent infractions, but like my old principal used to say, if kids get in trouble for chewing gum, they will not bring drugs to school. In other words, if we implement reciprocal consequences for the little missteps of home life, we might reduce the number of real-life consequences that will hit our daughters square in the face.

Having to Make Amends

Akin to replacing the melted carton of ice-cream is the concept of making amends for wrongdoing. I have often said if someone steals your car and then asks you to forgive them … but they want to keep the car … they have lost their mind. If the car is not returned, amends have not been made!

Obliging your daughter to make amends should be a standard rod in your discipline chest, but it is a little tougher than it sounds. For one thing, our society has bought into a "free grace" culture, which implies an unlimited number of free passes should be granted to anyone who requests forgiveness. Making amends goes against that grain.

Do you remember when retail stores posted signs that said, "If you break it, you buy it"? That concept has become foreign to our social conscience. One time, I dropped a glass jar in a store. Knowing good and well my carelessness led to the store's loss, I carried the label from the jar with me to the check-out counter so I could pay for it. When I tried to explain myself, the worker insisted on excusing me, saying, "That's what we have insurance for." I appreciated her grace, but I paid for it anyway.

Our daughters will do much better in this world if they believe behavior matters and that amends should be made for their mistakes. If your daughter plagiarizes half a research paper (note: this is a very serious matter of copyright theft), she needs to admit it to the teacher and ask if she can redo her work for half the credit. If she runs over someone's mailbox because of careless vehicle maneuvering, she needs to spend her Saturday fixing it. If she ruins her cheer outfit by washing it wrong after the coach has been very specific about how to wash it, she needs to work for a new one and miss any performances requiring that outfit (unless it harms the team enough that the coach wants to provide her a temporary replacement, but that's a "team" issue).

My point is simple. If your daughter recognizes what it means to "make amends" for wrongdoing, she will walk more circumspectly and conscientiously. She can learn from a very young age that her decisions will come back to bite her. If her behavior has bitten into someone else's property, then, she needs to understand the rod of discipline called making amends.

Lecturing

I was going to place lecturing in the dad behavior that brings frustration to a daughter, but as I look back over my own life as *Dad the Dean of Discipline*, I realize lecturing actually worked with my girls. I know my lecturing can be boring and repetitive, but if I waited for just the right time, my girls never seemed to resent a long teaching moment, even if it was all about scolding them.

Maybe instead of lecturing, I was actually *counseling*. That is what you would call it if I were helping anyone else who needed an outside perspective for their problem. With that view on lecturing, I thought we should include it as a healthy rod of discipline.

If you plan to use lecturing, just be sure to stay within the limits of normal human capacity to process information. As much research as has been done on attention span, I could not find definitive statistics to rule out lecturing as a useful mode of discipline. Even so, as your daughter's dad you should be acquainted with her attention span. You know her well enough to strike while the iron is hot and quit striking once it is cold.

Since you know her, you can be the conscientious lecturer who responds to verbal and nonverbal cues. You can use pauses and questions and honest reflection in order to get to the real heart of the issue where she needs you to bring correction. If a dad can do these things in his lectures, he can use lecturing as a beneficial rod.

On the other hand, if what you mean by lecturing is talking on and on because you love to hear yourself speak … or if you hope your incessant voice will wear your daughter's resistance down to the point of blind obedience, then lecturing will not work. In addition to that, if your lecturing is as one-sided as mine often was, leaving no room for flexibility and no ear for your daughter's response, then lecturing can go back up to the bad list in Principle One: Do Not Frustrate Her.

Leverage

This final mode of discipline is king of the rods. We will call it leverage. In the business world, leverage governs negotiations. Whoever controls the greater assets controls the dialogue. Even if a win-win settlement is the ultimate goal, the one who can make do on his promises or threats will be the lead figure in the room.

As Dad, you need to tally your assets and use them to your advantage. If you decide an asset will be leveraged in a behavioral negotiation with your daughter, you must hold out to the end. The dad who folds too many bluffs will find himself signing away his rights, forfeiting his influence as *Dad the Dean of Discipline*. However, he whose talk is not cheap but is backed up by real assets will leverage his way to real disciplinary success.

Leverage, then, begins with indexing your assets. The list should not take long to compile, and it will change from time to time. When your daughter is 4, your assets are different from when she is 14.

Your next task is to keep tabs on which assets matter and which ones do not. For one child, losing her TV privileges — an asset well within Dad's control — will amount to torture, but for another child, TV is not important in the first place. If you have a daughter whose main mode of entertainment happens to be hiding away with a book, you might resort to restricting her book time in answer to a behavior problem. You will appear to be taking away something that is good for her, but you must leverage it because it's the asset that matters to her.

I laugh when I tell people my parents must be the only parents in the history of humankind who took away my church activities as a punishment. When I was a teenager, my church youth group and certain ministry outreaches were my main thing. My parents knew where the jugular was, and they were not afraid to strike. That is called ruthless leveraging ... and it worked.

In our home, once our girls were beyond the toy stage, we kept a short list of our most valuable leveraging resources: allowance, weekend freedom, phone access, and car privileges. For easy reading, I thought I would break each of these four down on their own with simple examples and maybe a few warnings in case these sound like assets that will work for you.

Car Privileges

My oldest girl will tell you the way to stifle her smart mouth was to take away the keys to her car. To be dropped off and picked up like a 13-year-old put her on a quick road to recovery. Within a short time of realizing dad had not been bluffing, she found herself quite capable of self-regulation when deciding whether to sass her mother. Sorry if "sassing" is only a Southern thing, but whatever you call it where you are from, taking your daughter's car keys might cure her of it.

Just remember that most leveraging requires sacrifice on your part. This is why I am encouraging you to make a list you know will work for you. If your daughter's car privileges actually help your household run better, then think of another leveraging idea before you jump the gun.

Phone Access

Restricting phone access, another one of our major assets, sounds counterproductive since we needed our daughters to have their phones for safety. Nevertheless, taking their phones away while they were at home provided Mom and Dad incredible leverage. It is amazing how attitudes and behavior shift so smoothly when phone leverage is applied. Suddenly, she has no outlet, no media, and no apps. She will feel like she sold her left arm just so she could break a simple household rule or neglect her duties.

The examples of phone leverage opportunities abound. A phone is like a magic wand. Waive it over her homework, and the homework suddenly becomes important. Hold it until she spends a few constructive hours with her younger sibling, and she will make lasting memories. If you implement phone leverage wisely, you will negotiate win-win deals with your daughter. Everyone will benefit. It worked for us.

Weekend Freedom

When we took away weekend freedom, we called it grounding. Grounding always seemed like the easiest asset to leverage, but I found out the hard way it is one of the most difficult threats to back up.

No sooner had I grounded one of my daughters than suddenly I would be reminded that her best friend's surprise birthday party was this weekend. I am not keen on punishing other people for my daughter's dereliction of duty, so I would find myself recanting or rescheduling a grounding.

I mention this to highlight the fact that some modes of discipline require forethought. Anyone who walks into a business deal without his ducks in a row will walk out of the room having been taken. Do not get taken by too many "unforeseen" compromises to your disciplinary decisions. Your daughter needs the sting of consequences to be consistent in your home so she will be less prone to disingenuous behavior when she grows up.

If you are going to ground her for the weekend, be sure the cost to you and the rest of the family does not outweigh her original offense. Once you have grounded her, she needs to be grounded.

Allowance

Finally, on a positive note, allowance is a great idea for leveraging your influence over your daughter's development. Money (which we never had a lot of) is the asset of assets.

Googling the top ideas for how to apply an allowance system will bring up plenty to choose from. Whether you implement a system of tokens that change hands throughout the week to be cashed in every Saturday or if you just rely on a straight salary-style allowance with bonuses and demerits, money will play its natural role as motivator.

For several years, we kept what we called the "Allowance Log." This was a spreadsheet where the girls could record their chores and other allowance-worthy accomplishments. It even included a chart that detailed the monetary value of certain tasks around the house, like how much a load of dishes was worth or how much a girl could make by mowing certain sections of our acreage. They still had steady chores, but the per-chore allowance gave them something to lose by putting things off.

Besides chores, we also recorded the girls' book-reading on this allowance log. They recorded the title of each book they read along with its number of pages. The going rate back then was "a penny per page." Your kids will probably want a nickel, so you will not be able to afford it. Sorry.

The allowance log was a fun, rewarding rod of discipline. Payday required Dad or Mom to calculate totals for each girl and check off the PAID column on the log. The plus side for those of you with really bad kids, you could include penalties and fees in the chart and your children could wind up owing you money at the end of the week. Nice.

Final Notes

That is my take on being *Dad the Dean of Discipline*. Principles rather than rule books should guide us through this difficult position. If we can master the thinking behind the principles, there will be a lot less need for rules at all. Unbecoming attitudes, derelictions of duty, and disingenuous character can all be averted through careful thought and the implementation of a few proven rods of discipline.

When we think of our daughters' personal development as a positive goal and do our best not to frustrate that development, our perspective of "discipline" changes.

When we check our own motivations and leave our egos out of the equation, we can succeed with this life-giving role as disciplinarian and move on to the more interesting hats on our hat rack. Just before we slip on the next hat, however, I want to close with two final thoughts on the matter of discipline: 1) relationship trumps discipline, and 2) discipline is a team effort.

Relationship Trumps Discipline

Because so much "discipline" revolves around external motivators—and seemingly *forced* behavioral adjustments—I want to leave this chapter with a reminder that your personal, positive relationship with your daughter is your best course of discipline. To be certain, if we find a chosen mode of discipline to be causing more harm than good to our relationships, we must be quick to find a better solution. We might even need to apologize when a "rod" of discipline has proven ineffective and destructive to our relationships.

I know you do not want to be wishy-washy or change horses midstream, but if you have grounded your daughter for three weekends in a row for the same behavior and the only result is worse behavior, you might need to check your relationship with her before it is too late. If what you are doing is not working anyway, maybe at least you can save the relationship. Too many times our role as disciplinarian puts us in the position of "controlling" someone else's behavior, a concept all of us know rubs us the wrong way if we are the one being "controlled." Think about it that way and try to find an answer through the relationship you have with your daughter instead of through the disciplining techniques we have listed in this chapter.[9]

Our end goal for our children is to usher them into healthy, happy relationships with their world, and because of that, we must remember that our relationships trump any mode of discipline. Please do not allow your role as *Dad the Dean of Discipline* to drive a wedge between you and your daughter. Activate your powers of discernment and implement discipline in accordance with what you know will genuinely benefit your daughter in both the short and long run.

Discipline Is a Team Effort

And finally, *Dad the Dean of Discipline* does not need to do this job alone. If you are a single dad (or mom playing a dad role the best you can), I hope you can find help from your daughter's teachers, coaches, pastors, extended family members, and others. If you are married, talk this chapter over with your spouse. Your spouse and you are technically supposed to operate as one person. In the area of disciplining your children, this is even more important.

This book is not about marriage, so I will leave the rest up to you, but be encouraged: If you can team up with your spouse, serving the office of Discipline Dean will be much more rewarding and will make the next hat fit so much better.

The next hat is one which too many dads never don because they get bogged down in the long, drawn-out chapter you just read. When people think of good parenting, their thoughts often fixate on whether good discipline is being enforced, but there is so much more to this Daddy-Daughter thing, which you are about to discover as *Dad the Liberator*.

[1] *The Merry Wives of Windsor* Act 3, Scene 5

[2] *Henry IV Part 1* Act 2, Scene 2

[3] *Corialanus* Act 2, Scene 1

[4] *All's Well That Ends Well* Act 2, Scene 3

[5] *A Midsummer Night's Dream* Act 2, Scene 1

[6] Bob, et al. "Shakespeare Insults: 50 Shakespearean Insults & Put Downs." *No Sweat Shakespeare*, 10 June 2020. www.nosweatshake-speare.com/resources/shakespeare-insults/.

[7] Name changed to protect the innocent pastor.

[8] Just so you know, I do believe in the spiritual world of angelic and demonic beings. The point here is that the girl's moral failures did not originate from demon "possession."

[9] For the record, I do not believe in exercising "control" over another person. The very idea of discipline should lead to self-governance.

6

Dad the Liberator

Changing hats from the *Dean of Discipline* to the hat you will need for this chapter will take some real dad skills. Sometimes you will even wear these hats simultaneously, but technically, they are opposites. *Dad the Dean of Discipline* establishes rules and borders while the dad wearing this new hat pushes the envelope. He presses his daughter to the edge of the border and offers her the freedom to explore. Whenever your daughter is ready, try this hat on for size: *Dad the Liberator*.

The Rites of Passage

I mentioned in an earlier chapter I think the Holy Family must have had some of these skills. At the age when Jesus would have become a *bar mitzvah*, they apparently loosened the reins on him a bit. Their family album reveals that before he was 12, he went through the physical, mental, and even spiritual growth we would naturally expect for a child in a stable home. Then after he was 12, he was also allowed to grow socially. These two parents (about as perfect as parents can get) had a great handle on how and when to liberate their kid from the constraints of childhood.[1]

Every culture around the world seems to have some sort of passage ceremony or understood season when a young person crosses the plain to adult-likeness. As I mentioned in the story of Mary, Joseph, and Jesus, the Jews call this time the *bar mitzvah* (or for girls, the *bat mitzvah*). In Latin communities, young girls celebrate their *Quinceañera*. The Amish recognize Rumspringa as the time adolescents become old enough to choose their own lifestyle. Muslim young people become responsible for the requirements of Ramadan after they turn 12. The list extends as wide as the globe itself, but at your home, one day your daughter will begin to prepare to pass to new rights and responsibilities herself.

When that time comes, you will wear the hat of *Dad the Liberator*. As much as you have answered the call to be your daughter's border keeper, from this point forward, you will also need to be her border expander.

The Rights of Women

It is strange to me that Women's Lib is still a hot issue in our generation. I know the feminist movement might be plagued with the controversy of extreme pendulum swinging, but fundamentally, the idea that women and men should stand on level societal ground seems obvious to me. Maybe this is because I am the father of four women, but I would like to think it is because I am a level-headed realist. I hate that anyone ever had to start a "movement" in the first place. When I think of women having to fight for equality—right down to the basic right to vote—I have to wonder where the opposite, oppressive thinking ever came from.

I think the worldwide societal suppression of women largely came from patriarchal misinterpretations and mis-handlings of very holy writings. I'm not throwing the gauntlet down for a biblical debate; I just want to offer you a simple interpretation of God's creative intentions when "in the image of God he created them; male and female he created them" (Genesis 1:27b NIV). This account of creation makes it clear: both males and females bear God's image.

Besides that, as the story goes, when woman was cre-ated, she was given the title "help-mate," a compound word implying not only that she would be equal with the male (*mate* means equal) but also that she would be better than him in many ways (*help* means she had skills he did not). At least one Hebrew scholar believes if God had not insisted on compounding "help" with the equalizer "mate," then the implication would have lifted the second creation above the first.[2] Thank God for equality, right?

With that in mind, we raise our daughters with an un-derstanding of their God-given status as leader and lady. I could go on for days with the biblical argument, but suffice it to say within your little princess resides a powerhouse of potential. She can excel as the CEO of a Fortune 500 com-pany and still be the best mommy to her own little brood … if that is what she wants out of life.

If she is destined to be a biblical Deborah leading her country's armed forces into victorious warfare, she must learn to lead. If she is called to be a Mother Theresa, laying her life down for the least fortunate yet standing her ground against the male-dominated religion and culture of her day, she needs to believe her ear for God is as in-tune as any of her male counterparts. If her road takes her on adventures like Amelia Earhart, she needs to believe she can fly. If people need a cure only your daughter has the brain to come up with, she needs to believe in herself like Marie Curie. Throughout human history, women have set and exceeded bars of discovery, adventure, and leadership. Your daughter is one of those women.

Nevertheless, in listing these ladies as examples for your daughter to follow, I just played into a trap. I hope you will trip this trap, so your daughter does not get caught in its teeth. My list is a trap because the presumption behind it is wrong. Why would your daughter need only look toward historical *women* for examples of her potential? Why would I not also include a list of great *men* and how your daughter could break *their* records?

I hope you can get across to your daughter that she has a role to play that could be likened to anyone else's role, regardless of gender. She is a person, made in the image of God, called to do great things during her brief window on this earth. She has an obligation to respond to and prepare for the divine call of her own life. *Dad the Liberator* is here to expand her borders, teach her to conquer life, and inspire her to go beyond her dreams.

She Has to Trust Herself

Your first step as *Dad the Liberator* might be to convince your daughter to trust herself. She trusts you implicitly and has probably responded well to you as *Dad the Dean of Discipline,* but if you are going to help her stand on her own (which is the goal of the discipline in the first place), you have to figure out what it takes for her to trust herself as much as she trusts you. That means teaching her the process of discovering and following the right influencers throughout her life.

Many adults still struggle to find their own voice. Some might be able to point to a moment in their history when their voice was silenced or seemingly taken from them. They live most of their adult lives feeling their voice will not be heard. Be aware of this when listening to your daughter. Encourage her to find her own voice in that headful of voices and trust it.

Voices

She hears plenty of voices. Voices are one of those influencers your daughter will discover and follow. Sometimes the voices can be confusing. She might hear her best friend say one thing while her boyfriend says another. She might hear her teacher's voice challenging her, her coach's voice rousing her, the preacher's voice convicting her, or her mother's voice soothing her.

Deep in her mind, she registers all kinds of voices. Hopefully, most of them are like the ones in Chris Young's country song "Voices," where he hears his dad say, "Work that job, but don't work your life away" and his momma saying to "drop some cash in the offering plate on Sunday." After all, good voices offer good advice.

Hearing these voices must be—at least in part—how the conscience is developed. Teach your daughter to tune into the important voices of her life. She will learn to trust herself more as she categorizes the voices in her head. I know "What Would Jesus Do?" has been overused since the first WWJD bracelets were produced, but sometimes we still need to ask it of ourselves. Your daughter can tap the best consciences of the world by asking herself what others would say or do in her situation. This is the right way to listen to voices and eventually find her own voice.

Some would even say the voice of conscience is a spark of divine connection, letting us know God's best choice for our next move. Joan of Arc believed the voice she heard was divine, proved the voice to be accurate, and died for her commitment to it. Wherever the voice of conscience comes from, though, your daughter hears it. Learning to heed it is a key to her success and maybe even her survival.

The Flow of Concern

As *Dad the Liberator*, you can help her find her own voice. You can also teach her to follow her "flows of concern," as I heard one speaker put it.[3] Sometimes, for instance, the sudden concern she feels for her grandpa should probably be followed by a quick text to check on him. Who knows but that God put Grandpa on his granddaughter's heart because he really needed to hear from her in that moment?

Following the flow of concern can be taught. You might start by encouraging your daughter to turn her flow of concern into a prayer list. If something came to her mind enough to concern her, then she could turn it into a prayer. Praying for others, or even converting her own concerns into prayer, will get your daughter into the habit of trusting her flow of concern.

Finding her own voice like that could make a big difference for others. My youngest daughter had a flow of concern one night for one of her friends she had not connected with in a while. It was way past bedtime, but she had learned to trust this flow of concern, so she decided to text her friend. They spent some time getting back in touch that night.

A few months later, I watched a YouTube video where a precious young lady discussed her journey through insecurity. It was my daughter's friend.

Anyone watching the video would wonder how this beautiful young girl ever struggled with insecurity in the first place. Her Instagram account had almost reached "verified," and she was the epitome of a fashion model. As she tells the story, I am sure mouths drop to hear that one night she had planned her suicide with expert precision. Her letter was written, her hair and clothes were just right, her room was locked, and the pill bottle was turned up ... when her phone buzzed.

Yes, this was the night my daughter called her just to catch up. That night a family was spared a nightmare, as someone's "flow of concern" saved a life.

The Gift of Fear

A book I find myself recommending all the time deals with trusting your own voice. When I try to list the people for whom it should be a must-read, the list grows and grows until I finally throw out, "Everyone should read this book!" *The Gift of Fear* by Gavin de Becker opened my eyes in a new way to the importance of listening to the warnings of your senses, especially as expressed in the fears of a moment.

This book is especially poignant for dads of girls because it deals with the dangers our daughters can prepare themselves for by fine-tuning their adherence to "the gift of fear." In my house, we called this the Gift of Discernment and attributed it specifically to our ability to listen for the warnings God might be trying to send to our consciences. However you label this with your daughter, though, she needs you to help her tune into it. When she has a "bad feeling" about someone or something, she needs to learn to trust that feeling—and skedaddle to a safer place.

Without sharing details, I must at least tell you all four of my girls have dealt with stalker-level strange men. These men often had to be dealt multiple gestures of strategic rejection before they moved on to other targets. If you have a chance to read the book *The Gift of Fear*, you will be doing yourself and your daughter a huge favor.

Trusting Herself Is a Process

When you begin to see that you can trust your daughter to trust herself, you will know you are getting somewhere. Suddenly, you will find yourself saying, "I trust you to make the right decision," "I believe you know what you're doing," and even, "What do *you* think you should do?" Giving these affirmations will help her trust herself even more. As much as we talked earlier about walking her through social situations as *Dad, Communications Director*, imagine how proud you will be when you are finally *not* walking her through things anymore but rather just watching her walk.

That reminds me of how I taught our youngest girl to mow our two-acre front yard with a riding mower. She was young but eager to learn, so I did not want to hold her back. The only problem was that she could tear the mower up or hurt herself if she did not know exactly what she was doing. Therefore, I decided to test the whole process of full, partial, and no oversight. The first time, I walked beside the mower while she mowed (the *whole time* she mowed), pointing out the tree roots, sprinklers, and other obstacles to avoid. She did not feel very "trusted" (and it wore me out). The next time, I sat on the porch and watched her without letting her out of my sight. She still might not have felt like I "trusted" her completely, but we were getting somewhere. Finally, the time came when anytime the yard needed mowing, she could jump on the mower and go, even if I were not home. Not only did I trust her, but she had learned to trust herself.

Generational transfers of blessings and responsibilities rarely work out smoothly in our society. There is always a catch somewhere, and I think it comes down to trust. When successions of estate and business do flow easily, it is usually because *Generation A* made the effort to teach *Generation B* to be trustworthy, even to know how to trust themselves. More often than not, though, *Generation A* does not believe *Generation B* will ever be trustworthy, so *Gen A* decides to write a series of rules and regulations for *Gen B* to follow. That way all the traditions and customs of *Gen A* will remain intact with or without *Gen B*'s help.

This state of estate affairs is unhealthy for family lines altogether, but it is even more unhealthy between a man and his daughter. My daughters carry my DNA. Why on earth would I resist trusting them to be the very best versions of that DNA they could ever be? I want to trust my daughters as much as I trust myself, and I pray when this is all over for me, there will be four grown women who learned that they could trust themselves to live their best possible lives.

It's Your Decision, Baby

If we want the next generation to learn how to trust themselves, our educational system should offer accredited classes on decision-making skills, which is also the second step *Dad the Liberator* needs to take to teach his daughter to stand on her own. As an academic, I would never scoff at the focus we place on English, math, science, or history, but decision-making should rank up there with the big four as a core subject. Hands-on decision-making strategies should not be held off for adulthood.

By the time our kids are 25 and the decision-making regions of their brains are finally fully connected, it is a little late for their bosses or parole officers to offer them the simple techniques that would have helped them in their younger years before they had full access to their frontal lobes.

Lest your daughter enter adulthood like so many of her peers without an understanding of diligent, proactive decision-making, let *Dad the Liberator* deliberately teach them to her. You can find countless resources for teaching your daughter how to weigh all her options and set a proper course, but to get started, here is a short list of strategies we focused on in our home.

Pros and Cons

The most basic yet most often used decision-making strategy in our home was the age-old Pros and Cons List. We made our girls draw columns on a notepad and brainstorm every Pro and Con they could think of concerning decisions. Do you want to stay on the cheer squad, or do you want to join the drama department? Write the Pros and Cons of each. Do you want to keep babysitting sporadically, or do you want to get a steady part-time job? Write out the Pros and Cons. Do you want to go to that summer camp or make the trip with us to see your great-grandma? Let's see your Pros and Cons. To this day, if my girls have to decide between two good things, they will pull out a notepad and get their columns started.

A Pros and Cons List is a way to measure *good* vs. *bad* when it comes to your choices. A list like this lets you write all the *good* things about one of the choices in the Pros column and all the *bad* things about the same choice in the Cons column. *Do I want to go to this weekend retreat? Here are my Pros versus my Cons.*

If you are deciding between two choices, you will actually have four columns. Choice A will have its own Pros and Cons, while Choice B does too. When you are making the lists, you will find some of it repetitive, but stick to it. It is just a good way to get a visual on the potential ramifications of your decision.

This process will force your daughter to think things through. It will also prevent her from lying to herself when a decision comes back to bite her. She will always be able to look back at the list and say, "Oh, sure enough, that was one of the Cons." On a bright note, though, your daughter will make some very sound decisions if she learns to utilize Pros and Cons. One day, when your 17-year-old baby girl decides not to like a boy because he no longer looks good on a Pros and Cons list, you will find yourself hiding in the back room with your hands raised in victory whispering, "YES, YES, YES! Thank God for Pros and Cons!"

Priorities

Another method you can teach your daughter for making better decisions is to keep a short Priorities List she can use to measure all her commitments. If she is purposefully conscious of her priorities, she can make choices based on how each one fits in with her list. Her list does not have to rank her priorities from most important to least important. It just needs to offer broad categories of things that are genuinely significant to her decision-making. The list might look something like this:

- Relationship with God
- Immediate Family: Mom, Dad, and Siblings
- Extended Family: Grandparents, Uncles, Aunts, and Cousins
- Friends
- Health
- School/Education
- Extracurricular Activities
- Job

If she has a short list like this, she can put a plus or minus beside each one as she is weighing how every little decision might affect the areas of her life most important to her. This is the kind of thing she will make a habit of doing mentally, not necessarily on paper.

However, the list itself should very well be on paper, maybe even taped to her bathroom mirror. Having a Priorities List she has constructed herself will add to her wise choices day by day. If the list is written out and kept visible, it will always be at the forefront of her mind.

When she gets into a car and does not feel like buckling her seatbelt, but then she thinks of her grandma grieving at her funeral or her sibling sacrificing his college education to take care of her after she is disabled, she will click the belt for the sake of her priorities. When she is deciding whether to binge another season of her newest Netflix addiction, she might think for a minute about her job or her grades and turn the iPad off. The use of a priorities list will work its way into your daughter's psyche until great choices become second nature to her.

Goal-Orientation

Very similar to keeping her own heartfelt list of priorities, your girl will also benefit from learning how to make decisions based on predetermined goals.

All the popular self-help books detail how to formulate goals as overarching guides for building a plan and staying the course all the way to project completion. For this section, I thought I might list some of the books my girls have read and/or benefited from over the years. You will need to check the age-appropriateness for some of them:

- *The Slight Edge* by Jeff Olson
- *Mindset: The New Psychology of Success* by Carol S. Dweck
- *The 7 Habits of Highly Effective Teens* by Sean Covey
- *Do Hard Things: A Teenage Rebellion Against Low Expectations* by Alex and Bret Harris
- *Simple Steps to Impossible Dreams* by Steven K. Scott
- *Girl Boss* by Sophia Amoruso

Again, these are just a few books that made a difference in our daughters' decision-making skills. They are replete with principles of self-motivation and dream actualization. We never sat our girls down and had them write out a "mission statement" for their lives; I don't think we even instructed them on finding their life-goals, but these books showed them the basics of planning for success ... from making to-do lists to keeping their daily decisions oriented around a dream for a final product.

Intuition

Intuition is a tricky one, but the trickiness resolves itself if we uncover some of its cryptic elements. We often think of intuition as the mystical sixth sense, but I do not believe it is mystical. I believe intuition is simply the level of quick access we have to the information our five senses have already gathered. If your five senses store information on the hard drive of your brain's computer, then your intuition is your nervous system's RAM.

RAM is only useful if there is information stored on the hard drive. Sometimes when I am counseling a person, uncanny ideas come to mind that seem almost supernatural, like, "How on earth did I even think of that?" However, almost every time, if I take the time, I can trace the revelation of the moment back to a season of my life when the information was being burned onto my hard drive. I never knew during those seasons that this information would be so useful later in life as it flowed out in the form of intuition.

In this regard, intuition is akin to wisdom. If you have ever been around an old professional who seems to operate in an extreme level of intuition/wisdom, you have probably heard that same old guy say, "This ain't my first rodeo." Sometimes the guy who seems to have had all his dreams handed to him actually just kept plugging away in his craft until the parts and systems finally started clicking naturally. What appears to be luck or intuition is really just a load of experience finally paying off.

That is how intuition works. If you let your daughter in on your knowledge of the world and how it works, she will often appear to have wisdom beyond her years. People will ask you how she speaks with such authority and has so much confidence. You will say, "Ah, she just comes by it naturally," but you will know in your heart it's because you helped her explore, experiment, and experience things that were then stored deep within her for easy access when it came time for her to shine.

Dreams (a Subset of Intuition)

Exploring the subject of intuition, I want to share with you a small piece of my family's decision-making processes that might sound strange at first. As I said, intuition is like the RAM of a computer that accesses and assimilates the information stored deep within the mind. Because I have made a few big decisions based on this next phenomenon, I would be remiss to leave it out of a decision-making discussion. I am referring to the practical interpretation of nighttime dreams.

In our family, when one of us wakes up from a dream, rather than immediately dismissing it as free entertainment, we usually take a moment to think about whether the dream could be a clue to something else going on in our lives. Throughout history, world-changing inventions, creative works, and scientific discoveries have followed dreams that came unexpectedly to a deep sleeper. From the sewing machine to the periodic table to countless other creative breakthroughs, dreams have often helped people who were willing to listen.[4] Who knows what good things might be hidden in your sleepy lucidity?

The reason I think dreams are a subset of intuition, however, is that they work best when there is something in your brain to build on. You might remember the cupbearer's and baker's dreams in the Bible. Do you remember what their dreams were about? That's right ... cup-bearing and baking. Yet inside the dream was a deeper meaning for their immediate situation. This is how you explain to your daughter that intuition—and the intuition of dreams— works. She takes her conscious thinking as far as it can go, and then she sleeps on it. Intuition takes over from there.

Each of my daughters has harvested useful information from her dreams. One of my girls was encouraged through a dream to pursue an internship position that did not even exist at the time. The details of the dream are her business, but I can tell you the interpretation was for her to seek a position with a mentor who was not accepting interns at the time. Her dream turned out to be a key part of her decision-making process, and she landed the position with this prominent, sought-after mentor.

Another dream all my girls benefited from produced an exciting story we will remember for the rest of our lives. When the band One Direction was just becoming popular and all the teen girls across America were in love with these five boys, our local radio station broadcast a treasure hunt with clues that led to free One Direction concert tickets, complete with travel money and a hotel stay.

A few days into the treasure hunt, still no one had come up with the tickets, but one of my daughters woke up from a dream where the band had jumped out of a van to surprise her! In the dream, she saw certain landmarks and bushes, but when she woke up, she could not place them. She came downstairs to tell us her dream, and Mom said it sounded a lot like a park we had not yet thought to explore. We decided to take the drive, and yes, you guessed it, my daughter exclaimed, "This is it!" One of her sisters found the envelope taped to the bottom of a slide right there in that park. Imagine the blast these girls had knowing that somehow intuitive intervention helped them decide where to search for their treasure.

Ok, that one was a little more mystical than intuitive, but I had to tell the story because it is too cool to leave out.

The conclusion of the dreamy intuition matter, then, is this: encourage your daughter now to fill herself with all the book learning and life experiences she can handle. What she takes in through the scientific method today will flow out of her as intuition tomorrow.

If you can convince your daughter to lock away every lesson the world grants her, she will one day be the wisest of her peers. She will learn to use intuition as one of her decision-making strategies. Once she fine-tunes her intuition, it might appear to be a quick, innate strategy for split-second decisions, but we know the secret of the intuition mystery: intuition comes from a slow brew of deeply owned, hard-earned knowledge.

The 24-Hour Rule

Taking time to slow-brew brings us to another decision-making concept our daughters learned at home. You might not call this a strategy; it is more like a rule. When I first learned it from our daughters' softball coach, I immediately recognized it as brilliant.

Coach Sher was just Cajun enough not to care what parents had to say about her, so she boldly posted guidelines of how she expected parents to behave. The most classic one was the "24-Hour Rule." This rule should be required of every sports parent in America.

The rule's premise was that if you had a problem with a coaching decision, you were welcome to confront her, but there was one catch. The rule mandated that parents wait 24 hours from the time of the offense to the time they approach Coach. As I said, Coach Sher was not afraid of conflict; fear was not her motivation. She just happened to be smart enough to know the magic of time combined with a good night's sleep.

She knew that when a parent is steamed about something, they should cool off before they make decisions. Even in a case where a parent was not necessarily angry, it was still a great idea to let the issue settle before confronting it. If after 24 hours of stewing (or preferably praying), you still had the same feelings about the situation, then you were welcome to bring her the complaint.

Coach Sher's rule could be a fortune saver for you, me, and our daughters. How many times have we paid years of interest on a decision made in a hurry? How many salespeople make their living by convincing you not to leave their office until they get a commitment? They are trained to keep you from sleeping on it because they know "sleeping on it" is one of the most protective decision-making strategies available to mankind.

This concept is easy to teach your daughter, and she will reap its benefits for a lifetime. If you convince her that 99% of life's decisions can wait until the morning, she will avoid heartache and costs galore.

Form a few habits around this rule if you think it would be useful to your daughter. Be deliberate about discussing opportunities but postponing decisions until after the discussion has had time to work its way through her conscience. If she is choosing whether to paint her room red or purple, for instance, talk her through the pros and cons of each color and have her declare which way she is leaning, but then tell her, "Bring me your final decision in the morning."

It is that simple. Even with more important decisions, where you might want to make sure your own opinion is known, if you notice your daughter has agreed with you without her own real opinion being expressed, you might say, "I don't want you to feel as if you are only doing this because you think it's what Daddy wants you to do, so let's save the final decision until morning. That way, you will have more time to think about it without me in the room." Talk about giving your girl the freedom to think on her own! When you are deliberate about this rule, you are operating in your role as *Dad the Liberator*. You are teaching her to process her decisions with confidence.

In teaching this decision-making strategy to our girls, we would often say, "You don't go grocery shopping when you're hungry, and you don't make decisions when you're tired or angry, so take some time to process all of this and make your decision later."

Fresh Eyes

If decisions do not have to be made immediately, you can always teach your girl to fetch advice from a fresh set of eyes. I do not mean from taking a nap ... that would fit better in the "dreams" section above. What I mean is for her to find someone else who has experience with the situation she is facing.

What better decision-making strategy is there than seeking the guidance of successful people? Besides that, how honored do you think Grandma or Grandpa will feel when their granddaughter calls or visits to ask their opinion about a difficult decision? At the end of the previous chapter, *Dad the Dean of Discipline*, I suggested we should enlist the help of a host of others in the molding and shaping of our daughter's discipline. Here, the same list applies. Your daughter can find mentorship relationships all around her. You can help her learn how to approach these mentors for advice.

"Have you called Destiny to see what she thinks?" That is a normal question my wife and I ask a couple of our daughters who have developed a mentoring relationship with our senior pastor's oldest daughter, 15 years their elder. Destiny provides a great set of fresh eyes for them. Never mind that she holds a law degree from Duke, speaks three languages, owns her own business, and pastors her own church, all while building a family with her husband and four kids. Each of our girls has a handful of people like Destiny whom they call upon for an outside perspective.

Mom's and Dad's wisdom is limitless I am sure, but when a non-family voice speaks, somehow the message comes across more clearly—even if Mom and Dad have said the same thing a thousand times before. That is one of the double-edged truths of liberating your daughter to seek advice from others, who represent fresh eyes.

Fasting and Prayer

One final decision-making method we stressed with our girls might strike you as antiquated but has proven itself powerful in our family. It is also quite simple: Fasting and Prayer.

Even when our girls were young, we set aside seasons of dedication to "go without" something we would otherwise indulge in. They saw fasting as a chance to tell God he is more important to them than candy or their favorite TV show. That is a great reason to fast.

Other reasons to fast include our health, our spiritual clarity, or—as we are discussing here in this chapter—an aid to decision-making. When my girls talk about fasting nowadays, they usually mean they are doing without food or some sort of media for a set amount of time while committing their thoughts to prayer about whatever decision has been set before them.

When our oldest was a sophomore in high school, she no longer wanted to play softball. This might sound like a simple decision, but she had played since fourth grade and was on a championship team. Of course, she was not planning to quit mid-season, so she had plenty of time to decide for the next year. We talked about how this decision was too important to be based on the feelings of the moment, so she fasted for three days before making the final call, a call she never regretted.

A more dramatic decision she had to make later in life concerned the empty feeling she had during her first year of college. After spending a year at the college where her scholarship led her, she still felt out of place and had not found her niche. She decided to take a three-day break from food and distractions to see if she could get some clarity of mind. When the three days were over, I kid you not, a series of "coincidences" suddenly unfolded that led her to the university where she would find her new home and where she finished her bachelor's degree. Now she works full-time for that same university and is pursuing her master's degree. This all fell immediately on the heels of taking time to fast and pray.

Our third daughter had a similar experience. After graduating from Hillsong College in Australia and trying to decide where to spend the remainder of her undergraduate years, she decided to fast and pray. Her fast led her to a decision that contradicted her original thoughts, and she wound up back in America. This all happened just a few days before Australia reported their first case of COVID-19 and went on lockdown. From that point forward, the job market for non-Australians in the country took a decided turn for the worse. Callie Ruth could have become penniless in a foreign country, but fasting and prayer helped her make a clear decision to come home.

At 18, my youngest daughter's ASVAB score had secured her the job she wanted with the National Guard, and she was four days out from swearing herself in. She had columned out her pros and cons. She had sought after great advice from various perspectives: some would ardently try to deter her, while others were all for it. In a good way, she had leaned heavily on the experiences of one married couple who had found each other in the military and also found great success in retirement. The husband's military career had even opened the door for his current job with the FBI. In addition to seeking all of this advice, she also knew her decision had not been hasty, and it supported her priorities. It would even fit well with her main goals, like acquiring an education and traveling the world. That just about exhausted all the decision-making techniques we have covered so far.

However, four days out from swearing in, Sarah decided to fast and pray for three. When the three days were over, none of her other decision-making points mattered because suddenly a new light dawned on her. She did not forfeit any of her patriotism, yet she knew for sure she was not supposed to sign herself over to Uncle Sam.

I hope these examples encourage you to believe fasting and prayer could play an active role in your daughter's decision-making education. Combining it with the other decision-making strategies of this chapter has helped each of my girls make some difficult calls in their lives. I believe this combination has helped them become leaders for themselves and others. I know it will do the same thing for your daughter.

Lead, Girl, Lead

I suppose you have guessed by now I want my daughters to be leaders rather than followers. I am guessing your possession of this book says the same thing about you. Certainly, we want our girls to be good followers too, for what good is a leader who has never learned to follow? However, our ultimate goal must be for our daughters to be the head and not the tail, for them to know how to control a room, for them never to shrink from positions of responsibility. We all want our daughters to become leaders, so let's teach them to lead. Then, let's take it a step further and learn how to follow their lead.

As *Dad the Liberator*, you are preparing your daughter to do life without you, and there is no better security for you than knowing she would prefer to be in the driver's seat. As much as you might joke about getting off the road when your daughter finally earns her license, I hope your confidence will rest on how well you can trust her to drive.

Quite literally, I do mean *drive*. Driving is one place you can teach your daughter the responsibilities of independence and the preferential role of the leader. One of my favorite songs for dads of girls is Alan Jackson's "Daddy Let Me Drive." There is something about driving that you cannot feel when you are riding. I wanted my girls to prefer the feeling of being in control so much so that they would be the one driving while their friends rode along.

Now that I am done talking about driving, let that be metaphorical for every aspect of life. Let's encourage our daughters to be leaders wherever they are. If small groups form in your daughter's classroom for the "shared project work" her teacher has assigned, talk to her about voicing her opinion and not letting her grade fall prey to the loudest contributor. As she gains seniority on her sports team, encourage her to spur the younger girls on to work hard and act right. Even if she does not aspire to be the captain of the team or president of the class, she can still be a voice of leadership for the other students. She can even be a silent leader, always faithful to demonstrate a strong work ethic and a winning spirit.

Whatever her leadership looks like, she just needs to believe that leadership is a position she must take, not for her own sake, but for the sake of others who will benefit from following her lead.

And with that in mind, I thought I would note another great way to teach your daughter leadership: entrusting her with leadership in your own relationship. My daughters have been able to lead me in many ways throughout our years.

Find Ways for Her to Lead

This might sound superficial, but when my girls were old enough to stop dressing me in boas and tiaras, they led me into a decent sense of style. One of the pluses of having four girls is that you can stay up on age-appropriate dad clothes. One day my oldest daughter even pulled me aside to say, "We need to do something about your hair. It's too short, and it's gotta change." Now, when people try to point me out to others, the other person might say, "Oh, you mean the guy with the hair? You should have said that in the first place."

I am still not the coolest guy in the world, but at least I know my hair products and have given up my tucked ox-ford shirt and pleated khakis from 1993.

Take Her Advice

It is not just in fashion, however, where I have learned to follow my girls. My daughters do not mind helping me be a better person. That is what I should expect, I suppose, since I want them to be great leaders. Even in my relationship with their mom, my wife, they never hesitate to tell me if my tone of voice or line of reasoning is just plain wrong. They are as respectful as the day is long, which I appreciate, but taking their advice, I have been quick to apologize and keep my relationship with my wonderful wife wonderful.

Leadership like that does not come naturally, but if you deliberately comply with your daughter's advice on some aspects of life, she will begin to learn how it feels to lead. Besides just taking advice from her, though, you must look for other ways to develop leadership in your daughter and let her know that her leadership is worthy of following. Let's cinch the concept of being *Dad the Liberator* by talking about three more concrete ways we can offer our daughters positions of leadership.

Seek Her Specialized Knowledge

One way is simply to seek her specialized knowledge, sort of like me learning to dress better. When it comes to specialized knowledge, I am your typical Enneagram 5. Sometimes I think my calling in life is to be a free encyclopedia for my friends and family. I will spend hours and hours drumming up original ideas for someone just because they mention they would love to understand something better but all the old ways of learning it have not made sense. I would call this a curse, but I enjoy it, so that would not be fair.

Knowing this about me now, then, you might guess I prefer to teach others rather than to be taught, so letting my daughters lead is not always easy. How could I learn anything from these little girls who were put on the earth to soak up my know-it-all wisdom? Well, truth be told, I have learned to learn from them a lot, and they love to be the one who tells me something I did not already know. That is how seeking your daughter for specialized knowledge will teach her to be a leader. You are genuinely letting her lead when you ask her to teach you something you do not already know.

Maybe there is a project you would like to get done around the house, but you don't have time to research the details for yourself. Get your daughter to Google it and bring you what she learned. Have her watch a YouTube video and show you the step-by-step instructions herself. Ask her to research a subject and put it in a nutshell for you so you do not sound stupid talking about it next weekend when you get together with that new couple who apparently have a hobby you have never even heard of before. Sincerely, if you ask your daughter, no matter what her age, to teach you something she knows, you will have a new favorite teacher.

Make Her a Project Manager

Another way you can teach your daughter to lead by following her is to make her a project manager and let her delegate assignments to everyone else in the house.

Need the playroom cleaned out? You have a new foreman who can tell everyone what to do in a non-bossy, amiable way. Want to take a weekend trip for the family? You have a travel agent and tour guide right there in your daughter. She can plan every bit of the trip from the cost to the fun. Let her. Better yet, ask her to. Need to plan a party for your wife? Your daughter could be the event coordinator who meticulously follows a budget.

Do you see the potential your daughter holds within her? Give her assignments that put her in a position of giving assignments and her potential will have a place to develop under the safety of your watch.

Ask Her to Pray

Finally, I would say an honorable and privileged way to teach your daughter to lead—and to let her lead you—is to genuinely rely on her prayers. It will do something supernatural to your daughter's heart when you tell her what you would like her to pray for. It will do you some real good too when you find out God answers her prayers for you better than your own prayers for you. Hahaha.

Leading in prayer does wonders for people. The first time I remember being asked to lead in prayer, I was in the sixth grade. We were performing "Down by the Creek Bank," and one song opened with a prayer-monologue. I am sure I spent weeks memorizing it, but I did not realize the responsibility of it until the lights dimmed, the music lowered, and my voice was the only one in the auditorium leading this prayer (yes, this was a public school, but the statute of limitations has passed, so you cannot sue them). I am sure the audience of parents and grandparents thought it was a sweet little moment, just like all the other songs from the evening, but it marked my psyche indelibly. From then on, I knew if people lead in prayer, they are leaders.

I did not grow up in a religious home. My dad is not much on organized religion. Not many of my spiritual notions even move his needle, but I remember one thing that did. One year, our girls coerced him into driving a delivery car for their youth group's Thanksgiving meal giveaway. It genuinely touched him to take his granddaughters through some of the less fortunate areas of town to deliver much-appreciated turkey and dressing, but what touched him even more surprised me.

I overheard him telling the story to someone when he said, "You should have heard Bethany pray for these people when we dropped off those meals." I guess she was 13 years old at the time, but to him, she might as well have been a queen. To be able to pray out loud on command like that … that was a mark of leadership.

As *Dad the Liberator*, one of the greatest ways you can liberate your daughter is to teach her to lead in prayer. Being prepared to do so offers her a leg up in leadership. We can talk more about this in Chapter 8, *Dad the Guru*, but when your daughter believes that you believe her prayers make a difference, she will have all the confidence in the world, and she will overcome the issues this world has to offer.

Hold Your Hat … The Next One's a Doozy

If being *Dad the Liberator* did not force you to get prayed up, brace yourself because this next one is a doozy. As you have already figured out, raising girls comes with lots of issues. I wish we could all hide our heads in the sand and pretend the issues do not abound, but they do abound, and we cannot hide. If you were already getting ready to put your head in the sand, pull it back out because we have a new hat to put on. You are about to be *Dad the Issues Manager*.

[1] A good version of this story can be found in Luke 2.

[2] Cunningham, Loren, et al. *Why Not Women?: A Fresh Look at Scripture on Women in Missions, Ministry, and Leadership*. YWAM Publishing, 2014. Pp. 95-6.

[3] Denny Duron, Sr. a sermon

[4] Accessed 10/12/20: https://www.wonderslist.com/famous-inventions-inspired-by-dreams/.

7

Dad the Issues Manager

I wrote the previous chapter *Dad the Liberator* hoping we dads would do our best to break our own insecurities and help our girls walk free. Of course, we dads have to keep an eye on them because that is also one of the hats we wear—*Dad, Security Detail*. But holding on too tightly too long reveals we have not stepped through our own fears.

Eventually, we must walk them down the treacherous path leading past their childhood borders, but for some reason, we shirk the role of liberator and keep them pinned in. Something within us wants our kids to be dependent upon us. I am not sure whether their dependence just boosts our sense of security or whether we really love the tax credit we get to claim on our Form 1040, but for some reason, parents struggle with letting their kids go. If we parents do not overcome this urge to restrict them, several negative consequences will follow, including, but not limited to, our grown children's natural rebellion against our personal views.

When this happens, moms and dads sit on the sidelines wondering how on earth they lost control of the game. Everything they were trying to gain by being in control has now erupted into a young person demanding their own liberty with unhealthy extremes. One educational program labels the control-factor of parenting "helicopter parenting," where the parent insists on hovering close enough never to lose their parental influence.[1]

I think part of the battle for us dads is that we always think our little girls are too naïve to the ways of the world, so they must be protected. If you recall, we did discuss this briefly in *Dad, Security Detail*. When you are the agent in charge of protecting her, you take it seriously. Of course you want to protect your little girl from "the things of this world," but remember part of what we talked about protecting her from is naivety! To do that, we must become the one who dashes naivety against the rocks; we must become the one who is not afraid to discuss anything with our daughters.

Dad must be the one she feels comfortable bringing her issues to ... her own issues as well as all the issues of this world that might challenge and confuse her. To shock-protect your daughter for when she walks out from under your shelter, you have to put on this new hat ... *Dad the Issues Manager*.

Be Real

I was telling my friend about a candid discussion I had just had with one of my daughters when he exclaimed, "Man, that's what makes you a good dad; you're so real!" I suppose being real comes naturally to me. It should really come naturally to everyone, but we get nervous when things get "real," and we pull back for the sake of sounding pious.

I can put on airs as much as the next religious person if I need to be sensitive to someone else's conscience, but I am not going to live that way in front of my family in my own home. In my home, we are going to talk about the real issues of life because we are real people. I do not need my daughters to think their dad walks on some holy cloud above the thoughts that tempt them to be normal human beings.

That is where being "real" starts: realizing we are all made of the same stuff. One of the best things you can ever do for your daughter is assure her that she is not strange, but that you and she have a lot of the same feelings, struggles, and viewpoints. C. S. Lewis pointed out, "Friendship is born at the moment when one person says to another: 'What! You too? I thought I was the only one.'"[2] I almost called this chapter *Dad the Friend* for this very reason, but that would limit what I want to get across as a broader picture. Suffice it to say, if you would like your daughter to feel comfortable enough around you to discuss real issues, then you must be "real."

Real Requirements

What are the requirements for being real? I can think of a few things. For starters, you need *honesty*. If you cannot be honest with your daughter about your own struggles (not that you have to share the ugly details), then how can you expect her to be honest with you?

Next, I think being real requires a very good *memory*. Hopefully, you have indeed risen above some of the struggles of your youth, but if you have forgotten the struggle, then you have lost its usefulness. Dig deep back into your middle-school memory; surely you recall what it felt like in the lunchroom, locker room, and classroom. Certainly, you remember the feelings you had about your own parents, your own friends, or your smoking-hot science teacher.

Tap those memories because they are keys to another quality required for you to be real: *Empathy.* A dad must be able to imagine himself in his daughter's shoes. Seriously, it is a real challenge to walk in four-inch heels while your date gets to wear sneakers with his tux. Let her know you understand how she feels; if you cannot actually under-stand her, then lie about it (just kidding). She needs to know you are an empathetic person, Dad.

Finally, if you want to be a "real" dad, you need the duo of *humility* and *humor*. Life cannot be all serious. I be-lieve life is hard enough on its own without being serious about it 100% of the time. Humble yourself and laugh! I should write more about each of these qualities, but I trust you can define *honesty, memory, empathy, humility,* and *hu-mor* pretty well on your own. Let's make them a real part of being *Dad the Issues Manager.*

What Issues Are We Talking About?

Before we go any further, I guess I should clarify which "is-sues" I am suggesting Dad needs to help manage for his daughter. A brief overview of the hot issues of the day will not hurt us, but please stick around to the end where we come back to the idea of how to talk about these issues with the young ladies growing up in our homes.

These are the issues we will not be able to shelter our daughters from. Sooner or later, they will run into every one of these issues. Oftentimes, their run-ins happen way sooner rather than later. Every issue we will discuss below will find its way into a PG-13 or TV-14 movie. Most of them are even introduced under the PG rating, and I am sorry to say so, but G ratings are not immune to some of these either.

I know it is scary, but your daughter could be made aware of every one of these issues by her classmates as early as kindergarten. I am not suggesting that you discuss them with your kindergartner; I am simply saying we have no idea what other kids are bringing to the table when our daughters sit with them at lunch.

Here is the short list in no particular order. You might want to call Dr. Phil for the long one. He has dealt with way more issues than I have. Some issues might weigh heavier with you than others, but I have tried to cover every issue I know you will have to manage at one point or another while your daughter is in your home.

Alcohol and Drugs

We might as well start with a biggie. My daughters found themselves in the same room with marijuana by the time they were freshmen in high school. I was blessed with girls who insisted on passing instead of taking hits and who made their escape from parties when alcohol and drugs arrived, but they still saw it all.

One day, when we were walking in a public place, one of my girls said, "Dad, do you smell that marijuana?" I was like, "What? I don't even know what marijuana smells like." Luckily, their mom is not as innocent as me because she was able to say, "Yep, somebody been smokin' a toke."

Sorry to make light of this, but I point it out to let you know you need to discuss the ramifications of drugs and alcohol with your daughter early in her life so when she is introduced to it, she will be prepared to make the right decision. She needs to hear the voice of *Dad the Issues Manager* in her head having already told her how to manage this issue. How you manage it is your business, but please be the main authority influencing how your daughter feels about drugs and alcohol. If you open the topic early enough and have real discussions about it, you will build a strong resilience in your daughter's heart to uphold your family's standards.

Left unchecked, this issue can take your daughter down a dark road, but if you bring the issue into the light, your daughter could at least turn into the permanent designated driver instead of being passed out in someone else's back seat.

She might even be the one who keeps the younger kids from veering off the better path. You would think all kids would want to lead each other the right way, but this is sadly not the case. Peer pressure is still alive, well, and as negative as ever in our society. When one of my daughters had just gotten to teen-hood, an older, very cool girl from her school promised, "I'm gonna be the one to get you drunk your first time."

Lucky for me, my girl had a rebellious streak in her, one which bucked when someone else tried to exercise control over her. I am grateful she and her sisters also bucked drugs and alcohol during their youth.

Sexuality

Another issue you cannot avoid is sexuality. This topic is so wide I do not even know where to start, but I know it has remained taboo for far too long as a family-time discussion in our homes. Your daughter has questions about sex you need to prepare to answer. Even if you need your wife to be the one who first explains the biological functions, you can only block and detract from all the other questions for so long. If she catches bad vibes from you concerning the matter, she will go silent at home and become a mystery of unknown thoughts herself.

In our chapter *Dad, Security Detail*, we listed some of the methods predators use to seek out vulnerable victims in their chat rooms. One of those methods is to hint about sexual matters as if he understands her better than anyone else could. Please do not let that happen! Also, be aware that online predators are not the only ones wanting to find out how your daughter feels about sexual matters. She will be thrown sexual inquiry from all sorts of directions. It is your job to help her be conscious of it.

Please be the dad whose daughter comes straight to him with what she saw at a friend's house on the computer and how it made her feel. Be the dad who balances the emotions and hormones that flowed from her brain to her body when she saw it. She might not even know how to feel. Is she supposed to be afraid? Then why does she also feel infatuated? She kinda feels both, and now she is confused. You are about to step up as *Dad the Issues Manager* who explains that sexual attraction is the most powerful attraction on earth, and she should not be surprised (or ashamed) that she has sexual feelings herself.

Even if she has attractions to certain people with great magnetism about them and wonders if this is telling her something about herself, you need to be the one to clear it up for her. You need to be the one who reveals to her the reason all the advertising around us works is that we humans are all attracted to sexual things. You must be the one who explains how she will be free one day to exchange sexual commitment with someone else. You must be the one who lets her know her sexual feelings in one moment or season do not lock her in to one person, to one lifestyle, or to one mindset.

If you do not want to be the one to offer "real" answers for her feelings, just remember someone else will be happy to. Do you want her to get her core sense of who she is from someone else's bag of answers?

You might be very settled on what you know is "right" and "wrong" about sexuality. I am fairly settled too. However, when the issues come up, you will do better as skillful manager than as all-knowing judge. If you believe your authority on the matter should never be questioned, you may get your wish. It will never be questioned … out loud, at least. It will certainly be questioned, however, in her lonely hours when her body, mind, and spirit have viewed contradictions to your rules in the lives of others who seem fulfilled and happy.

Part of being real is being open to discussion. That does not mean you have to bend your morals; it means you show her that your morals have not been etched into a stony heart with no feelings of its own.

Death and Dying

In my job, I have faced death and dying with hundreds of families. It is the highest honor of my calling to be with someone at their moment of passing and walk with their family through the grieving process. Because of the intense concentration of the subject matter in my life, my girls had a strange advantage growing up. They had been to more funerals by the time they were 10 than most people attend in a lifetime.

That sounds like a strange thing to say, but without having had those experiences, I can see that death and dying would be a difficult subject to broach in any home. How do you introduce the topic? How do you field the many questions your daughter might have? How do you know you are right? These are only some of the challenges you will face trying to discuss this subject with your daughter in a sober but natural manner.

I do not know of only one "right" way to address the subject. Nevertheless, there are a few wrong ones. To ignore it is dangerous. To be flippant about it will cause lifelong offenses. To dwell on it can lead to unhealthy fears and darkness. No one expects others to be experts on this subject, yet they are sensitive when it comes up and they are quick to be offended when someone else approaches the subject in a way they perceive as wrong.

Maybe that is the first lesson our daughters need about death and dying—*to know the whole world faces it differently*. Even though so many people see it differently, however, no one escapes it. That must be the second lesson: *Death is unavoidable*. Another lesson our daughters might learn is how people facing death need others to be near them. They might not need anyone to "say the right things," but *they need the comforting presence of their friends and family*. This lesson would be called *compassion*. Each of these elements of reality will come up at some time in your family.

You might not have the opportunity to attend random funerals and hear the different ways people celebrate their departed loved ones, but a few occasions will be offered to you organically. If you simply follow along with your natural surroundings, there will be no need for a deliberate curriculum to teach your girl about death and dying.

One perfect opportunity occurs every now and then when you pull your car over for a funeral procession. What a perfect moment to talk with your daughter about where that hearse is headed, how the family must feel, and where the deceased person might be even though his body is in a casket. Just turning the radio off and asking the family to sit quietly as the procession passes might create the reverence you need for your little ones to realize death is a serious matter.

Another way to bring the subject up naturally is to talk about older people, how they begin to slow down, and how their bodies lose their youthfulness and begin to head back to the dust. Your daughter's awareness that her grandparents will not always be here can be a healthy motivator for how she prioritizes her family time.

Finally, whether or not you find a natural way to discuss death and dying with your daughter, sooner or later she will face the issue. This world is a cruel place where children leave far too soon and tragedy takes the ones we love. If you can bring yourself to it, be the dad who alleviates some of the fears associated with death and dying. At least be the dad who is willing to talk about it.

Politics and Religion

It might offend someone to see politics and religion here in the same category, but these two subjects are psychologically intertwined. For good reason, most of us are raised to avoid bringing politics and religion up for discussion unless we have been invited to a legitimate debate.

Politics and religion will quickly drain any comfort out of an otherwise relaxing evening with friends. He who insists on violating this social precept winds up being "that guy," the one who "started it all." As all the other people leave the party, he feels as if he really brought life to the discussion, but the can of worms he opened left everyone else with high blood pressure. What was going to be a fun evening turned into a long drive home for spouses fuming instead of reminiscing over the evening's events. We should all know better than to be that guy.

Even though we know not to be that guy at a party, however, sometimes we need to be that guy at home. If you do not know where you stand politically or religiously on any talking point, let your daughter know you do not care enough about it to have an opinion. She will appreciate the freedom to have her own opinion or to realize she is also not required to have one. However, if you do know where you stand, she needs to know that too.

In the next section, I will reveal some of the approaches and attitudes that helped us in our home, but here I just want to bring the subject up. Your daughter's teachers, pop-star heroes, and friends will all have their outspoken take on politics and religion. She will need her hero at home (that's you, *Dad the Issues Manager*) to have some thoughtful positions of his own. Again, no dad is required to be an expert on every religious and political matter, but you do need to help her find her way around the reasoning of other people's political and religious views.

Cultural Norms

Everyone's worldview is limited by experience. Our socioeconomic station, familial upbringing, region of residence, and hundreds of other factors mold our perspective from the time we are born. Remember that classic optical illusion of the young lady/old lady? If you have never seen this drawing before, you eventually will, and upon your first look, you will either believe it is a beautiful young lady with a feather in her hair looking away from you or you will see an old worn-out hag. This "inkblot" drawing was designed to challenge our perspective and demonstrate how everyone has their own. How we see it might or might not say something about us psychologically.

I do not know about your personal psychology, but what I do know is we all see the world from different eyes. *Dad the Issues Manager* is here to help his daughter understand the various perspectives in our melting pot society (or "cultural quilt" as I think they are learning to call it today). In our home, when cultural norms came up for discussion, my goal was to reduce judgmental attitudes and increase healthy levels of godly tolerance.

Throughout her upbringing, your daughter will view many cultural norms that do not resemble what she has learned to call "normal." You have the unique privilege of broadening her experiences to fine-tune her perspective. Even if you do not see it on the surface, just like the other concerns your daughter is facing in her private thoughts, cultural issues are weighing on her mind. She wonders about the ways people live in cultures different from your own. She wonders why some older people in your town use the language they do to refer to people who are different from themselves. She is confused to hear some of the prejudices coming from her own family or even the pulpit of your church. She wonders where you stand when it comes to people of different races and cultures.

You are the one who has to make it clear to her. I pray your clarity draws a picture of a beautiful world as God would see it where "every nation, kindred, tribe, and tongue" would live in harmony.[3] You might not have put too much thought into it before, but now you have a daughter whose view you are responsible for, so you might need to talk to God about how you should see these things. When you get your answer, share it with her.

Money

I keep thinking our list of "issues" might work its way down to something less controversial, but here we are at another humdinger: Money. Money is a big deal. Money can blind a man all the way to his grave. It causes as many divorces as infidelity and strangles people's dreams when it amasses itself against them in piles of debt. Money can come between families, wedging them into silence for decades.

One time, I began to pull the I-pay-the-bills-around-here card on my daughters when suddenly I realized money should never be held over their heads as a means of manipulation. After apologizing, I assured them that for the rest of my days, they would own a key to our house, and it would always be "our" house. When you look at all these issues about money, I suppose it does need to be one of the number one issues a dad helps his daughter understand and conquer.

How do you see money? Is it the "root of all evil" or is it a tool to build your destiny? How you see it matters to your daughter. Maybe you do not feel equipped yourself when it comes to money. Sincerely, if you, like so many others, were thrown into adulthood without understanding your credit score, the power of compound interest, the ins and outs of insurance, or the fundamentals of the free market, then you of all people know the misery of feeling like you are coming from behind. What you and I can do for our daughters is make sure they get a head start.

My wife and I never saved a dime during the first years of our marriage. I am not telling you how many years because it is embarrassing, but I can tell you this: even though I did not have any money set aside, I taught my girls to save the second 10% of every dollar they ever make (I say "second" 10% because, in our house, the first 10% goes to charity).

Without fail, from the first time they ever earned allowance, they learned to set their savings aside for their future selves. If they made $10.00, they immediately understood that they really only have $8.00 to spend. This was simple to implement, and by the time my girls were heading off to college, each one of them had a nice little cushion (probably bigger than mine, but that's not saying much).

I share that little detail about saving money just to bring the whole subject into the light. Money discussions can make or break a family. Decide how your money discussions are going to sound. Decide if you want your daughter to take a personal finance course from someone like Dave Ramsey, Suze Orman, or another personal finance guru.

When I conduct premarital counseling, I take young couples through some of the basics of financial responsibility found in these types of programs. Every couple who has followed through with the concepts of saving, investing, and staying out of debt have found themselves in wonderful financial shape within just a few years of marriage. Every time that happens, I feel like my wife and I are getting a little bit of redemption from our lack of early financial smarts.

You can have that same feeling with your daughter as she grows older. Whatever financial mindset you decide to give her, if it sets her up for a better future, your daughter will thank you when she is old. And when YOU are old, she will be able to build you a cottage attached to her own house so you will not have to move to a nursing home.

Education and Academics

When you think of how your kids are going to be rich enough to take care of you in your old age, your first thoughts might immediately jump to education. Even if you are not one to worry about yourself as a decrepit old man, you still probably have educational goals for your kids.

Social class does not seem to matter when it comes to this issue of parenting. Wealthy, middle-class, and poor parents alike have a solid idea of what they want for their kids' educational future, and most kids spend their lives hoping they can please their parents academically. With that said, Education and Academics certainly fit the bill as an "issue" for *Dad the Issues Manager*.

We talked a little earlier about setting out clear expectations for our daughters so they will have a better chance of hitting the mark. With education, this can get tricky. It can be tricky, first, because of the various learning styles and number of learning disabilities that abound in our society.

Let me interrupt myself by mentioning my wife. She spent seven years as a therapist for kids with learning challenges. She has helped kids with every type of hang-up — ADD, ADHD, dyslexia, dysgraphia, Tourette's Syndrome, auditory processing disorder, and more. Through mental exercises and academic therapy, kids under her care with all sorts of problems learned to excel in school, overcoming their difficulties and sometimes even remapping their senses to better fit their academic abilities. In addition, my wife and I are associated with a center for autism, which proves every day that students with incredible challenges can function as happy, productive kids when someone helps them inch their way toward change.

I digressed to those examples because as parents with big dreams for our kids' education, sometimes we are faced with things we never expected. Furthermore, part of being a great dad to your daughter will be to assess where she stands academically. No matter what challenge presents itself to your daughter and your family, you can stare it down and give it a challenge of its own. You can determine to help her be her very best no matter what she has to fight.

Her "best" brings us back to the issue at hand. All our daughters can do academically is their best. The farthest they can go educationally is the farthest they can go. And, barring any laziness, your daughter will pursue excellence if that is what you expect. Then again, her expectations also play a part in this, which is why we have brought this up as another reason education is an "issue."

Many aspects of education will arise in the discussions of your home, and your daughter will appreciate your openness to find out where she sees herself educationally. My girls have done fine academically, but they have each run at their own pace in educational pursuits. My first daughter jumped right into a traditional college degree, changed her major and her university just like any normal American kid, and will soon have a master's degree.

My second girl gave up a full ride to a traditional degree to pursue three years at a ministry school that is not academically accredited. After those three years, she entered an associate's program at a community college. She has not regretted a moment of it.

My third daughter also had scholarships available for traditional school but was offered an opportunity to study abroad, where one year turned into three, and her trajectory shot far from traditional.

Then there was our fourth, the one who decided against the army but would have sooner traveled in a van across America than live in a dormitory at a traditional college for four years. She wound up taking a "gap year," working hard, traveling a little, and settling on a plan to get more traditional at a university.

I am not recounting my daughter's academic tales for any other reason than to press the issue that each of our girls is her own person. Each of them will find success in this world. I know they will because I know them. Their mother and I could have pressed each one of them to follow the expected path to the four-year degree and a career, but we wanted each of them to know they had made the decisions for themselves. We discovered what they wanted for themselves by allowing academics and education to be an "issue" worth discussing rather than a standard everyone is just destined to keep.

The List of Issues Goes on and On

I am tempted to make this list of issues a mile long. If I did, however, I would just be rehashing other parts of this book. How your family views social media, for instance, is a huge issue. Another issue is your family's perspective on *luxury* versus *necessity* or *work* versus *leisure*. You might even need to come to a consensus on the difference between laziness and rest, balance and complacency, healthy food and the average family's diet. Indeed, all sorts of lifestyle questions might become "issues" for *Dad the Issues Manager* to manage.

Then there are even the relationship issues your daughter will find herself in. What kind of friend will she be? Will she have a "best" friend, or will she have several people who are each "one of her best friends"? If she is allowed to have a "boyfriend," how do you traverse the ramifications this will have on her other friendships? These would be too many issues to read about in one sitting, so you—*Dad the Issues Manager*—can just keep your list open to add more to it as you go.

So Now We Know the Issues ... But How Do We Deal with Them?

As you get your list going, your next step will be to decide on your managerial style. What we need is a brief *Issues Management Handbook (IMHB)* with a few easy rules. A handbook guides a manager when his vision gets cloudy and his judgment is skewed by personal feelings.

I tried to keep the following guidelines in the forefront of my mind while the "issues" of life came up for discussion in our family. We spent countless hours around the island in our kitchen talking things out, seeking each other's opinions, discovering compromises, and just being real with each other. See if this managerial handbook helps you and your daughter along the way.

IMHB RULE #1: Seek her opinion and feelings.

I have experienced a strange phenomenon as a pastor that has opened my eyes to how people perceive each other. I hope I can explain this well. Situation: someone asks to sit with me for "advice" on a personal matter. We spend the next 45 minutes together, and I might only speak one or two sentences. Actually, that is an overstatement. Oftentimes, all I do is nod my head and interject little phrases to let them know I am still listening.

After a long "discussion," the person feels relieved. Later on, I hear back from them or someone they know, "Pastor Brian helped me so much" or "He knew exactly what to say." I think it is so funny because I know I hardly spoke a word. They feel as if I offered profound wisdom, yet all I really gave them was an ear for their own opinions and feelings.

That is the first rule in our handbook: *Seek her opinion and feelings.* Ask her to explain herself. Remember, at this point of following the guidelines, all you are giving her is your ear. It does wonders for a woman's heart to have someone willing to listen!

Listen well enough to paraphrase her words back to her. I cannot tell you how many times I have repeated back what I thought I heard one of my daughters say only to find out I had not caught what she meant. Seeking her opinion means keep asking her for clarity until you finally understand it.

If you do not like her music but have never asked her what she likes about it, then how will she ever know you value her tastes? If she is frustrated with the financial freedom other families seem to enjoy, while your family is always pinching pennies, try not to reciprocate her frustration. Instead, seek to understand the root of her fears. Heck, aren't you frustrated sometimes too?

Regarding every one of the seven big issues we have already opened in this chapter, seek to know your daughter's opinions and feelings. Ask her where she thinks she stands.

Another way to discover where she stands is to ask about her peers. I am not suggesting that you pry into her friend's personal business with constant questions about their weekend activities. Rather, ask her what the consensus is among her peer group about the most recent current events.

Ask her, for instance, what level of sexual experimentation seems normal in her generation. Ask her how her friends might be dealing with the fears of school violence. Ask her how her friends come up with all that extra spending money. Listening to her talk about her peers will open your eyes to her perspective. You might be pleasantly surprised to find her swimming against the stream, or you might get busy finding a way to intervene before she jumps on board with a bunch of careless teens heading toward destruction.

When you discover where your daughter stands on certain issues, you might find yourself at odds with her. As your daughter becomes more aware of the world outside your home, she will feel at odds with you too. So there you go; you have issues. She will come home from school, church, or someone else's house with all kinds of issues to manage. If home is the place where her opinions and feelings find value and maybe a little validation, you will win your daughter. If you read her questions as a challenge to your authority, you will lose her.

Evaluating what she has brought to the table requires a level of honor between the two of you that has been built through years of your position as Dad playing all the roles we have talked about in this book. Try not to forfeit all your efforts now just because the issues have become less controllable. You are still *Dad the Issues Manager*.

Just remember as you listen to her, everyone goes through their own evolution of thought. You have been through yours and she must go through hers. If you hope for her to evolve your direction, seek out her opinions and feelings. And above all, do not run her off by rejecting them. The next rule in our Issues Management Handbook should help with that.

IMHB RULE #2: No knee-jerking.

Let's talk about your poker face. As much as I pride myself on being open to talking about anything and everything, my face still flushes pink when certain subjects come up. I never think of myself as embarrassed, but I sure look embarrassed. Even if I am not uncomfortable with the subject matter at hand, the blushing itself embarrasses me. It is funny, but I hate it for myself.

If I could control it, I might be a better poker player. As it is, however, if I am holding a royal flush at your poker table, you could easily read my face and know to fold. I do not bluff well either, so if I look like I am lying, I am. Just call my empty hand and rake all my chips into your lap. That is the way poker goes for me. However, when it comes to protecting my daughters' hearts, listening to their opinions and feelings, they will get a poker face from Daddy. I cannot react with shock or anger. If their fear of upsetting me drives them to secrecy, we are about to lose all our chips anyway.

The opposite of a good poker face is the knee jerk. When the doctor hits your patellar tendon with her little rubber mallet and your quadricep contracts involuntarily, you demonstrate a healthy knee jerk. This sign of a healthy reflex system must be one of the oldest medical confirmation tools known to mankind, but a knee-jerk response to your daughter's newfound opinion about some political, moral, or social matter is dangerous!

When your daughter tests your reflexes with her unexpected rubber mallets, you must overcome your natural tendency to knee jerk. *Dad the Issues Manager* can handle a few hits to his patellar without overreacting. If your daughter has seen or done something that has riddled her conscience with questions, you cannot let a sudden knee jerk throw your foot into your mouth.

My friend Marc Pittman, author of the memoir and soon-to-be movie *Raising Cole: A Father's Story*, implemented a parenting protocol that speaks perfectly to the no-knee-jerk policy of our Issues Management Handbook. Marc's book details the principles of his relationship with his sons, one of whom, Cole, was taken tragically in a one-car traffic accident on his way back to the University of Texas after a weekend home with his family. Marc called this parenting provision "Dead Man's Talk."

His promise to his boys was they could call for Dead Man's Talk anytime they needed him to listen to them with no more reaction than a dead man would give. He was offering them the confidentiality that would require him to take information to his grave. Marc says this "would allow me to steer my boys away from pitfalls, instead of trying to rescue them after they'd fallen in."[4] His description of how it played out regularly with his sons offers a good picture of how to listen without knee-jerking:

> Cole was seven and Chase was three when I introduced the concept of Dead Man's Talk to them … I told them they could tell me anything. That could mean anything they were doing or thinking of doing, anything their friends were doing or thinking of doing. Whatever they told me would stay with me. No matter how much I wanted to punish them for it, I couldn't. No matter how much I wanted to lecture them, I

wouldn't. That didn't mean I wouldn't explain the consequences of their actions or intended actions, or remember it and maybe use it to shape what I would teach them or how I'd try to influence them later. But I made certain they understood that what they told me during Dead Man's Talk only I would ever hear.[5]

As you can imagine, such a commitment between a dad and his sons opened the door for some very private discussions about the issues of life. I never implemented a Dead Man's Talk with my daughters, but I always strived to watch my reactions closely, offering my girls a safe place to confess their issues without a knee jerk from Dad.

"Confession" might sound extreme, but this word gives us a final analogy of the comfort we offer our daughters when we give them our ears without an emotional response. Priests hear confessions from trusting parishioners with no more reaction than to offer forgiveness and a plan for recompense. I do not think you should don the white collar and build a confessional for your discussions with your daughter about life, but offering her the same nonjudgmental reactions she would get from a priest would certainly make her more comfortable approaching you about how she feels.

When you approach her as *Dad the Dean of Discipline*, she knows some consequence is coming for her behavior, but if she approaches you as *Dad the Issues Manager*, she needs to feel the comfort of a dad who can help her sort things out … with no knee jerks. That is why we need this rule so badly in our Issues Management Handbook.

IMHB RULE #3: When possible, AGREE.

Rule #3 goes back to our need for a "same team" mentality between us and our daughters. Any chance you get to affirm your daughter's positions, take it. One of my friends taught me a valuable parenting lesson that applies perfectly to this concept: "Say *yes* as much as possible so when you say *no*, it will sound like you mean it."

He was referring to granting permissions to our kids, but I have broadened the idea to how I "grant permission" for my daughters to think for themselves. When your girl hears "no, no, no" as your normal response to anything she asks for or presents to you, she will hesitate to approach you with anything. She might even resign herself to the notion one of my brothers often proposed when we were growing up—*Do not ask for permission now ... Just ask for forgiveness later.*

Yikes! I do not want my daughter to think like my brother! Therefore, I will find a way to say "yes" to her beliefs on as many matters as possible.

Occasions will always come when you can't agree with her completely. That is when you ask yourself if you can at least relate to part of her position. Please do not be shocked by this next example, but one of my girls went through a phase where she wavered in her patriotism. We are talking about a girl who has proudly sung the National Anthem in front of thousands of people at statewide sporting events, but one day she began to question our allegiance to this system so riddled with flaws. You might agree with her, but forgive me ... I still get chills when I hear Lee Greenwood or Toby Keith sing about the flag. Besides that, I read the

Declaration of Independence all the way through every 4th of July.

Nevertheless, I listened to every grievance my daughter brought to me about our current problems in America. I agreed with her that they are *real problems*, even systemic problems. Moreover, I encouraged her to keep prayerfully pondering all the ramifications of her new thoughts. About a year later, as she donned a red, white, and blue shirt in a foreign land to make sure everyone there knew where she came from, I beamed. She even said to me, "Whatever problems we have, we are still the greatest country on earth." That evolution might not have happened if I had put my hands over my ears and blurted out The Pledge of Allegiance to drown out her viewpoint.

If you can grant partial agreement to your daughter's concerns, if you can temporarily suspend your stubbornness in order to hear her out, if you can play the devil's advocate against your own views, your daughter will appreciate it.

She will find her own voice. She will grow in confidence and feel less threatened when you disagree with her or "put your foot down." She will be free to believe in herself, and she will be much more prone to believe in you. It takes faith to trust the grand paradox: what you fight her on, she will fight to keep, but when you release her to think for herself, she will likely think like you! After all, she is your daughter, so if you can agree with her on an issue, do it.

IMHB RULE #4: If you come to an impasse, call in a favor.

The simple fact that she is your daughter can be your ace in the hole, but you must know how to play it. Remember, you have always been *Dad, her First Love.* Also, you have done well as *Communications Director* and *Security Detail.* She has appreciated these roles you have played in her life. Regardless of the roles, though, you have been Daddy all her life, and one day you will be Granddaddy to her kids. What I am saying is she loves you, admires you, and genuinely cares about your feelings. These can all play in your favor when you and she clash on an issue and reach a stalemate. Let me explain by restating the IMHB Rule #4: *If you come to an impasse, call in a favor.*

If what I am about to say sounds like manipulation to you, then this rule will not work for you. You must be able to see the purity in the motive or you will not be able to set the stage for implementing the rule, for asking the favor. With that said, however, if you approach it with a genuineness of spirit, your daughter will respond in kind and you will successfully traverse some issues that could otherwise hurt your home's harmony.

What is the favor? Simply put, you ask your daughter to suspend her conclusions until a later date. You call upon the old logic, "You might not agree with me, but I need you to follow the rules of this household." You do not express this sentiment in anger; rather, you lay it out as a call to her free will. If, for instance, she does not agree with a certain precept of your religion, you ask if she can wait a few more years into her independence before she nails her 99 Theses to the doors of your church.

If you have shown yourself faithful with the other rules in this handbook, I can almost guarantee your daughter will comply with your request for a favor. I have often said to my girls, "I know how you feel about such-n-such or so-n-so, but you still have my last name. Please honor the way you know I would treat the situation." They have never hesitated to grant me such a favor because they know my heart is in the right place.

If, in your worldview, you know you are right about an issue, and you cannot find room for compromise, you need to ask her for this favor. Let's say, for instance, she wants to lash out at her school administration for a controversial decision they have made, but you need her to respect their position of authority because honoring authority is a standard you cannot allow to be compromised in your home. In this case, you might have to call in a favor. You will not convince her the administration was correct, but you can ask her to honor your principles. She will.

She will honor your principles when she feels honored by you. She might not adopt all your opinions after she discovers her own, but even if she has seen a different light, she will be willing to honor you while she is in your home. If you do not want to call this a favor, then call it something else, but somehow you must convince her to temporarily suspend her viewpoint.

Look back through the list of issues above: sexuality, the role of alcohol in society, the value of money, our different approaches to death and dying. Every one of these issues might present a gridlock in your relationship, but every opinion concerning each of them can also be suspended until further knowledge and experience are acquired. Your daughter will understand this. *Call the favor in.*

Ask her not to settle her opinion too soon and not to jump on any bandwagons until she is really ready to go.

Your presentation is the key. Honor her with the acknowledgment of how she represents you while she is under your care. Let her know you are proud she bears your name. Encourage her with the promise that you will be happy for her to call her own shots when she is truly on her own. She will make all sorts of concessions for the daddy who has made concessions for her. Daddy just has to be real about it.

Closing Thoughts on Issues Management

We opened this chapter talking about what it takes to be "real" as a dad. As mentioned earlier, some of the most relatable qualities a dad can exhibit are honesty, empathy, humility, a far-reaching memory, and a good sense of humor. If you need laughter, use it. If the sensitivity of an issue brings tears to your eyes, let it. If you can recall your own evolution through the issues of life, let it build your empathy. Use everything you can get your hands on to build your daughter's character and help her find her voice. If a YouTube video says it better than you ever could, then get her to watch it. If you find out her favorite pop star has similar parental feelings as you, capitalize on that.

Pray for wisdom. Pray for patience. Pray for perfect timing. *Dad the Issues Manager* has some tough issues to manage. If they get tough enough for you, prayer might become your number one tool. Hey, you will need every tool you can find. Even if nothing else in this whole book helps, tapping the Divine will.

If you know how to pray, you have a shot at being the best dad ever. A dad who has a heart for God will always win his daughter's heart. That is why the final role you play while your daughter is under your roof is *Dad the Guru*, walking with God through your journey as Dad.

[1] Fay, Jim. *Helicopters, Drill Sergeants, and Consultants: Parenting Styles and the Messages They Send*. Love and Logic Press, 1994.

[2] "91 Motivational C.S. Lewis Quotes on Friendship, Heaven & Love." *OverallMotivation*, www.overallmotivation.com/quotes/cs-lewis-quotes-friendship-heaven-love/#:~:text=%E2%80%9CFriend-ship%20is%20born%20at%20that%20mo-ment%20when%20one,it%20is%20the%20very%20sign%20of%20His%20presence.%E2%80%9D.

[3] Revelation 7:9

[4] Pittman, Marc, and Mark Wangrin. *Raising Cole: Developing Life's Greatest Relationship, Embracing Life's Greatest Tragedy: A Father's Story*. Health Communications, 2004. p. 54

[5] Ibid, p. 52

8

Dad the Guru

We finally arrive at this chapter. I promised in Chapter 1 I would eventually get to my "thing," the thing which holds everything else together for me. I implied it had everything to do with faith, and it does. Even as I tried in the other chapters of this book to stick to general principles that should guide any dad on his journey with his daughter, I have not completely masked my spiritual views from you. To be sure, my choice of language and various allusions might have given you the proper assumption I am a believer. I hope thus far my faith has resonated with you as a real thing and not just a "thing" that might or might not help. Being a believer and walking with the God I believe in has made me the dad I am.

Right upfront in this chapter, which draws from deep within my spiritual beliefs, I would like to acknowledge at least one atheist I know who raised two wonderful daughters of his own. I do not know his whole story, but I know his daughters well. They are both tremendous people who contribute to their worlds with love and compassion. One of them has even turned toward faith and credits her parents for the freedom to believe, which she experienced in their loving home.

Another dad I know as a "non-believer" is one of my dearest friends on earth. He has raised a daughter who

would make anyone proud. I point these dads out to validate the fatherhood of men from every faith—or non-
faith—background.

Whether or not they had the same faith as me, these
dads did a great job.

Faith Made All the Difference for Me

Certain elements of my parenting would not have made it
into this book had I not had faith. My walk with God presented me with advantages I can only describe as divine, so
it might not even be fair for me to leave this part out. Sometimes it was as simple as the calming factor of a faith-filled
prayer as I placed my hand on the crown of my daughter's
head. Other times, it displayed itself in an inner voice letting me know where my daughter's heart needed the most
care, or which of my daughters might need me most in a
moment. Faith highlighted these simple moments all the
time for me.

Truly, it is only right for me to include the importance
of faith in some of the most trying moments of being a dad
to my girls. My relationship with God got me through the
night an irresponsible ER doctor blurted out that my
daughter's migraine symptoms "could be" signs of multiple sclerosis. Without the faith to pray through that night, I
might have fallen apart. Thankfully, the potential diagnosis
was off base, but I did not know that at the time. That night,
I prayed myself hoarse waiting for the sun to rise so we
could visit a different doctor.

Another example of my dependence on faith dates back
to my first day of becoming a dad. I was in the hospital caf-
eteria with my best friend, taking a break from my wife's

hard labor, when an alarming word was sent down for me to return to the birthing room. When I arrived, I saw what can only be described as panic on the nurse's and doctor's faces. The baby's heart had stopped under the pressure of the present difficulties and they were not sure the baby would live.

In that moment, a prayerful utterance roared out of me that was not even English. It rose from deep within this young daddy's heart and probably scared the doctor even more than the situation we were in. When I placed my hands on KaLyndia's belly as the nurse and doctor looked on, I swear power came through me that was not human. Suddenly, the monitors lit back up, the doctor grabbed his big set of baby grabbers, the nurse jumped on my wife's belly like a WWE wrestler and pushed with all her might, and a living daughter popped into this world ready to meet a dad with a little bit of faith.

Because of the myriad Divine moments that marked my household over these years, I am now compelled to include this hat on the hat rack for you. If you will try this hat on, you will find that the rewards exceed your hopes. Put your faith to the test a minute, and read on, Dad. Here is your new hat: *Dad the Guru*.

How Is Dad's Spiritual Life?

Sometimes dads relegate this area to Mom. Mom is the one who prays. Mom is the one who tells the kids about God. Mom is the one who reads Scripture to them. I am sorry to break it to you, Dad, but if faith is going to be a part of your household, then your daughter needs you to show her a little bit of *Dad the Guru*.

No one is asking you to preach like Billy Graham or to starve yourself like Gandhi. Neither do you have to pronounce blessings like the Pope or wear a tunic like the Dalai Lama. However, you do need to walk with God in a way your daughter can see it. Does she hear you pray? Do you refer to how God would expect us to treat our neighbors? Do you honor God verbally and request guidance for yourself and your family? Do you at least say grace at mealtimes?

I hope some of those questions challenge you to search your heart for the answers because for the rest of this chapter, I want to talk about becoming a spiritual leader for your daughter. I pray you will read these next passages with a hungry heart for the spiritual strength faith can give you. You might already be a person of faith who seeks God with all your heart. If so, you will find the practicality of this chapter helpful. However, if you have not yet taken your own steps toward God, I pray these pages will inspire you to run in that direction.

I am sharing my faith with you not because I think I have it all together but because I know I have just enough of it together to have made a real difference in my daughters' lives. After all, that is what this book is about—wearing whichever hat is necessary for each moment of raising your daughter. In many moments, you will need to wear the hat of *Dad the Guru*.

The Spirit, Not the Letter

When I talk about a relationship with God, I am not referring to a set of religious standards adhered to or an absolute creed confessed. Do I require certain standards of myself and my family when it comes to morals and integrity? Absolutely. I hope the previous seven chapters of this book make a sharp display of that.

However, I have taken great care to categorize the standards of our home in a way that does not put religious-sounding lingo on them. You might remember one of the "Frustrating Errors" committed by *Dad the Dean of Discipline*: Religiously based corrections can do more harm than good. That is why I believe we should watch closely for our relationship with God to be a genuine pursuit and not a religious goal.

If I set a standard for myself that sounds righteous but is not true to God's Spirit, it will backfire on me. If my relationship with God is denominational, for instance, then instead of talking to God concerning a religious matter, I will simply refer to the tenets of my church's doctrine. Hence, I close the door to relationship because someone else has already told me how God feels.

Moreover, if I refuse to talk to God about the science of the created world and instead resign myself to an ancient version of a sacred passage that seems to contradict science, I am caught between siding with the God who created science or with the way God's people have viewed the world for thousands of years (i.e., the earth is flat, etc.).

Furthermore, if I align all my political affiliations with a group who claim to speak for God because none of their own number has had the courage to contradict them, I am not displaying a relationship with God. Instead, I am indicating that my spiritual life is subject to the dictates of other men. All of these are simple examples of how we can sometimes default to rules or dogma instead of seeking God personally.

I summarize this dilemma with a concept called "The Spirit, not the Letter." "The Letter" represents anything you might follow to the "T." If you want your cookies to taste the same way every time, for instance, you measure the ingredients right down to the milligram. You follow the "letter" of the recipe. For more examples of following the "letter of the law," look to sports and games, where rules and boundaries define the game.

These are instances where the "letter" often outweighs the spirit of the rules. You never hear a basketball referee say, "Well, when they wrote this manual, they didn't really intend for 'out-of-bounds' to imply you have to turn the ball over. We can let the Red Team keep the ball just this once." No! Sometimes, the letter of the law is the final say.

However, some principles of walking in faith supersede the "rules." Jesus pointed these moments out with simple illustrations. His own Bible, for example, said a person could not do *any* work on Saturdays—*none*. That was the rule, and anyone who broke it would be shunned, not only by his neighbors but ultimately by God. Yet there are always those times, Jesus said, when your donkey might fall into a ditch on a Saturday.[1] Anyone who leaves his donkey in the ditch a whole night because of the rules might come back the next morning and find a dead donkey.

These are the situations where you don the hat of *Dad the Guru* and prove yourself willing to ask God for God's preference ... *God, would you prefer a broken rule or a suffering donkey?* This is what the Bible refers to when it says, "For the letter kills, but the Spirit gives life" (2 Corinthians 3:6 NIV). Should I follow the Spirit or the Letter? *Dad the Guru* discovers which is which by walking with God deliberately.

My daughters needed to see a dad with an authentic, dynamic relationship with God. I am sure they would also benefit from a dad who was smart enough to know exactly what he believes on all the nuances of faith, but they needed more to know their dad was not afraid to talk to God, to expect God to answer, and to be willing to follow God's leading no matter what that meant. This is what I hoped to be as *Dad the Guru*.

Pray for Her ... Pray with Her

Dad the Guru knows how to pray. That is you. I already know you know how to pray because you know how to talk. To pray is to talk out loud when no one else is there to hear you except God ... and to believe that God is there to hear you. When you do it enough, you will begin to have thoughts bounce back at you as if in reply. Well, they will be something like thoughts anyway, but really, they are a deep understanding that God is answering.

So how do you turn this concept of prayer into being *Dad the Guru* for your daughter? You pray for her! Unless you are in this habit already, you have no idea the effect it will have on your daughter for you to say, "I prayed for you this morning" or "I stayed up late last night and talked to God about your situation."

Imagine even further the moment you pause with her before she gets out of the car and you say a simple prayer that God will help her with her classes, her relationships, her upcoming game, or whatever else you know she hopes you care about. Your daughter's deepest needs are sometimes hidden inside the part of her heart only she and God can see. I promise she wants to know her Dad sees them too.

I am not trying to simplify this concept to make it sound childish. Sometimes when you pray, you need to know you are fighting for your daughter as if a genuine war has broken out over her soul. Sometimes you will say things to God you might not want her to hear, yet you must say them to God because prayer is the way God operates.

I have prayed for my daughters' eyes to open when I think they are walking blind. I have prayed for their hearts to soften when I know they have suffered the pain of bitterness. I have prayed for their attractions to change so they would shift their attentions away from a boy who I know is up to no good! God has answered these prayers in ways that could only be called miraculous.

To be *Dad the Issues Manager* and confront my daughter on any of these topics might turn out okay, but it also might lead to disaster. On the other hand, to be *Dad the Guru* and pray for her privately will spare us the confrontation and make a bigger difference in the spiritual realm where mountains can be moved by faith. "Prayer Changes Things" might just sound like a cute bumper sticker meme, but it is truer than any other bumper sticker you have ever seen.

The Prayers of Job, a Great Dad

No doubt you know the story of Job. In our culture, "the patience of Job" has become a cliché. We all know he lost everything yet never turned his back on God. One thing you might not know, however, is what a great dad he was. If anyone was ever *Dad the Guru*, this man was. Ironically,

Job's story occurs chronologically before any organized religions ever existed, so his walk with God was real. It was not a religious show.

About how great a dad he was, though, get this. Job was a very wealthy man, so wealthy that his grown children were able to live in leisure. They often held parties for their friends and kept late hours. This, of course, is not what made Job such a great dad. What made him great is his habit of prayer for his kids.

Rewind the story to the decades before Job's tragic demise and you will find a man who took his family's spiritual condition very seriously. Job rose early in the morning to pray for his children and their families. The story tells us this man regularly offered sacrifices to God on behalf of his children "just in case" they had fallen short in their character. In other words, he bore a personal burden for his children's right standing with God.[2]

Can I do that? Can I sacrifice my own time and humble myself in prayer for the sake of my daughters? What does that look like? It looks like a dad who knows how to pray. It looks like a dad who believes God is his ally in his battle to be the best dad his daughter could ever dream of. It looks like *you* … when you approach God in faith.

If You Do It, She Will Too

Let's say you take this challenge. Let's say you begin to believe a communication line between yourself and God has somehow been left open. Let's say the more you talk to God, the more you feel like doing right things and the more you begin to think thoughts that could only have come from a source outside yourself, a Source of genuine love and goodness. If that is the case, then you must be putting on the hat of *Dad the Guru*. Of all the important hats you wear, this is the one she will want to share. Yes, when your daughter sees God's Spirit in you, she will want It too.

And so, we reach the "parenting" side of all this spiritual talk. As *Dad the Guru*, your spiritual walk means taking your daughter with you. As we mentioned in *Dad the Liberator*, your daughter can learn to fast and pray as one of her decision-making processes. This is something *Dad the Guru* demonstrates and teaches. She can learn to follow God's leading. *Dad the Guru* helps her meditate on God's character so she knows what that leading feels like.

Now we are delving into even more aspects of her spiritual growth. *Dad the Guru* will teach his daughter to serve God by serving her fellow man. If she becomes God's hand and voice to others, it will be because you showed her what that means. If she grows to be a generous giver, it will be because *Dad the Guru* dug deep for the causes that moved him.

If your love for God is genuine, then your daughter will follow you in your chosen mode of worship. She will even follow you into becoming responsible for her own conscience. The fact is, within a short time of seeing Dad's spiritual devotion, your girl will most likely outpace you in hers. If you are willing to be *Dad the Guru*, you will be surprised how close she follows you in her walk with God.

Her Developing Spirituality

I must emphasize one more time I am not talking about being *Dad the Dogmatic One*. I am talking about being Dad who walks with God. If I did not want to walk with God, I would leave my daughter's religious development in the hands of the experts, or I would leave it off completely. I would send her off to Sunday School and hope they get it right, or I would tell her not to trust anyone with religious ideas because they might be trying to manipulate her. If I did not have faith myself, then her spiritual development might scare me. It is certainly a heavy responsibility even when I do have faith.

Lucky for you and me, we have daughters. They have faith. Something about them just seems to know there is a God and makes us believe in God too. Jesus' disciple Mary is a great example. Scripture notes that she "sat at the Lord's feet" (Luke 10:39 NIV). This phrase indicates she was "in school" with Jesus; she was pressing hard to discover the spiritual elements of life that would help her be all that she could be.

Your daughter's spiritual hunger is important to God, even as Mary's was. Jesus said of Mary, "She has chosen what is better, and it will not be taken away from her." For your daughter, you will be called upon to help her choose what is better in her spiritual development.

Vetting for the Better

Unless you are raising your girl in a commune with no access to the outside world, instances will often arise for her to hear about spiritual matters from other people besides you. That is when *Dad the Guru* might have to vet the spiritual influences who vie for your daughter's attention. Vetting is a heavy responsibility.

Since this book is for dads, there are many instances where I seem to be putting all the parenting onus on you,

Dad, but I have not meant to imply that. Let me interrupt myself here to reiterate this important point. Unless you are in this on your own (Single Dad), then these responsibilities are born on two sets of shoulders, not just yours. Your daughter's mom is as much a guru as you. In this matter, especially, I feel compelled to make sure I mention your spouse. This whole parenting experiment is a team effort, especially things as serious as vetting her spiritual influences.

Sometimes vetting means you just need to keep your eyes and ears open. My girls have always had great Sunday School teachers and Youth Group leaders, but I still listened closely to make sure my daughters were catching the right concepts from the spiritual leaders of their lives. If I noticed something my girls might have misunderstood or something a young teacher said that I thought was inaccurate concerning spiritual or religious matters, I could teach my girls to "chew up the meat and spit out the bones," so to speak. If you listen well enough, you will be able to vet people and information this way.

Other times, you might have to vet someone in a more literal sense. If your daughter wants to attend a summer workshop, for instance, to learn how to "flow in prophetic worship"—or any of the newest catchphrases these days—you might ask around about the place she hopes to visit. Your pastor, for instance, might have insider information on the character of the people in charge.

You might peruse the website of the place she wants to go. You might even call someone from the organization and see how you feel about them. How you feel about them over the phone might tell you all you need to know. This is the kind of vetting *Dad the Guru* might do to help his daughter mark the path for her spiritual growth.

Provide Checks and Balances

After you have vetted the spiritual influences of your daughter's life, you might also want to prepare yourself to offer her some checks and balances. When I was 16 years old, I became so "fired up for the Lord" that I would run through a wall if someone told me the Bible said to do it. One time, I actually did put my hand through a wall … all because my brother would not agree with me about what was right vs. what was wrong "in God's eyes."

When I confessed to my dad what happened, his response checked me. He looked down at the steering wheel of the tractor he was driving and said, "I knew this would happen if I let you go to that church." For the record, my anger issue was not my church's fault, but the point I want to make here is clear: Even though my dad would never have called himself *Dad the Guru*, it was his job to check my passions and balance my positions.

Young people are designed to run hot. When your daughter tastes a moment of frustration about the injustices of this world and how God wants us to sacrifice our lives to change them, she might want to drop out of school and join a mission or a movement. It will be *Dad the Guru*'s job to draw her back to her home mission. When she comes home from a weekend retreat and has decided no one in the house is allowed to watch TV anymore because the preacher there said it was "sinful," you might have to remind her God can use a TV as easily as he can use that preacher.

Make Your Red Flags Count

I am not implying that you will always be at odds with the zeal she acquires from her spiritual experiences. I hope, on the contrary, you would add to the passion of her journey's exciting moments. I would even warn you not to come across as questioning and judging everything she gets enthusiastic about. In fact, as you did when you were *Dad the Issues Manager*, you might practice saying "yes" as often as possible so your red flags will make a bigger impact when you have to wave them.

If you have to wave a red flag, that is when your relationship with God comes into play. Because I was not afraid of this hat—*Dad the Guru*—my girls grew up believing my spiritual and religious opinions held weight. Your girl wants to see that in you. She yearns for her *First Love*, her *Security Detail*, her *Dean of Discipline*, her *Liberator*, and her *Issues Manager* to lead her in a solid spiritual walk, which gives her confidence with God.

When she knows you walk with God, her confidence in you will make her sensitive to your red flags.

Believers Believe for the Best

As you can guess from the relative brevity of this chapter, I do not like to press my religious beliefs on people. I just hope I have said enough here to inspire the believer in you to believe. As I bring this concept to a close, I would also like to note that God wants the very best for you and your family. If you pursue God, you will see this as clearly as I see it. Sometimes it is easier to see it for others, so maybe that is why I see it for you, but while you are wearing the hat of *Dad the Guru*, it is part of your job to see it for yourself.

When my girls were still young, probably not even in grade school, I ran across a verse in the Bible which jumped off the page as if it were mine. I hope you have had experiences like that. The passage itself was not exactly mine. It actually fit a dad named Phillip. The verse says, "This man had four maiden daughters who prophesied" (Acts 21:9).

Well, here I was a young dad with four little girls in his home, and I wanted them to "prophesy" (i.e., to grow up to speak for God). Naturally, my wife and I wanted the very best for them in every way, not just spiritually. We wanted them to grow up happy and provided for. We wanted them to dream big dreams and learn to love like champions. We wanted all this and more, but most of all, we wanted them to live for God. So when this verse jumped out at me, I decided to print it out and frame it. It hung on the wall of my office all the years these girls were growing up.

I did not preach it to them or demand it of them. I just believed it for them, and here I am writing a book about them. They grew up. They made it. And now, the proudest moments of my life are to hear about the ways they love and serve God.

I began this chapter with an apologetic tone because my sensitivity to everyone's religious differences gives me pause. Indeed, I would have considered leaving *Dad the Guru* off the hat rack altogether if my faith had not been so significant to my daughters' views of me. Of course, I do concede the title of the chapter is a little facetious, but if naming the hat *Dad the Guru* makes the point stick with you, I am glad I did it. If you want your girl to get the whole gamut, you have to realize *Dad's Faith Matters*.

No, I would not call myself a *Guru*. However, I did do my best to *believe*. If you believe the best for your daughter, I think she will make you as proud as mine have made me. As I said at the beginning, I have always been proud to point toward one of my girls to say, "I'm her dad." That was the case when they were two years old and heading to the nursery without making a fuss. It was the case when they headed off to start their own lives thousands of miles away from me. That will always be the case as long as I am here on the same planet with them, and if my faith is right, it will be the case when I stand before God to answer for the job I have done.

Between now and then, though, I do not think I am finished being Dad. I might not wear all the same hats, but there is one more hat I suppose I will keep on until it is all said and done. That is the final hat we will talk about, *Dad of the Future*.

[1] Gospel of Luke 14:5

[2] See the book of Job, Chapter 1

9

Dad of the Future

I just spoke to two grown women about their dads. I asked them to tell me about their grown-up relationship with their dad so I could look into my future at what kind of dad I need to be as my girls get on with their own lives. One of them almost cried as she remembered her dad's tough demeanor and harsh disciplinary practices at home. She said many things that all came down to, "I can't tell you a lot; I feel like I spent my whole life waiting for his full approval."

Her dad is gone now. She did get to have some precious moments with him, but his full approval never came. One beautiful footnote she added, however, brought my mind back to *Dad, her First Love*. She says every now and then, she pulls out an old four-line poem he jotted in her autograph book when she was eight years old. She reads it through to remember that her dad must have loved her because he wrote her a poem.

The other lady I spoke to had a similar upbringing. She explained bluntly, "My dad beat the daylights out of me." She added, "I never knew how to deal with that as a grown woman until my pastor talked to me about honoring my dad even though I don't like him. That helped me because I could not make myself like my dad."

Later in life, this lady's relationship with her dad changed for the better as they worked to get to know each other. Then when he came down with Alzheimer's, things changed even more. As sad as Alzheimer's is, a silver lining shone through her dad's condition. Since he could no longer remember how badly he had treated her, she was able to lay it aside too. She cultivated a new relationship with her aging, forgetful dad, a relationship where he thought of himself as a loving father and she could return the feeling. That might sound strange to you, but think of what it says of your daughter's heart. She will still need you to be her daddy well into the future.

So far, this book has been about those 18 to 24 brief years when your daughter is climbing her way through childhood and into adulthood. That is the part of being Dad to daughters I have already experienced. So far, so good, but I still have a long way to go with this dad thing. That is why I could not feel comfortable closing things out without one more hat that awaits its wearer: *Dad of the Future*. In other words, what kind of dad will I be to my grown daughters?

Giving Her Away

During the months I was writing this book, I was also in the middle of preparing for a wedding. My Bethany Grace had found the man of her dreams and was ready to start a new life with him. By the time I got to this chapter, the day had come and gone. I walked her down an aisle, gave her a final kiss, and "gave her away" to a fine young lawyer who will be a great partner for her. What a proud moment. Since I am *Dad the Guru*, I also got to perform the ceremony, so that was neat too. I only mention all this here because I have to remind myself this event was only a milestone; it was not the finish line.

"Giving her away" seems like it would mark the end of fatherhood, but I cannot imagine that to be the case. Do not get me wrong … giving her away was a huge moment. From the moment a daughter is born, all the other moments feel like they are leading to that big day. Education, of course, is a big deal. Discovering her career? Yes, that is colossal too. But the day she signs her name into another man's heart … that day is the one dads of daughters look toward with a bag of mixed emotions.

I cannot tell you how many times I have heard, "You better be saving money! Those weddings are going to be expensive!" Again, even in the minds of society, the wedding day is the big day … the day Dad takes on a new role. I am still wondering what that role will be. I have seen some dads do a pretty good job of being Dad to their grown-up daughters, and that gave me an idea.

Since I do not have the experience of my own, I did the next best thing. I sent word out to several of my grown female friends to see if they could share ideas about what has made their dads great dads even into adulthood. The following pages are what I gleaned from these daughters' contributions. Their insights will help us all be *Dads of the Future* for our little girls when they are not so little anymore.

Insights from Grown Daughters

Life revolves around relationship. Sadly, many relationships are so broken that some people live in perpetual frustration. They seek fulfillment but hit walls of bitterness.

They fall short of healing because their forgiveness formula never balances evenly on both sides of their justice equation. In my world as a pastor, I regularly observe relationship-breakdown. At any given time, someone, somewhere needs to talk about a relationship that has fallen apart. Relationship friction marks a normal quality of life for far too many people in our world.

For others, though, life's orbit around relationships is a joy. A grown-up daddy-daughter relationship is supposed to be one of those. Just like all relationships, it will have its ups and downs. It will not be void of trial, but if it is healthy, it will balance itself out. In other words, it will be mutually beneficial: Daddy and Daughter, both fulfilled by the roles each other play now that she is grown.

To find out what sort of mutual benefits grown women with good dads have discovered in their adult years, I sought help from several women whose viewpoints could prove valuable to us dads inching our way toward the future. These ladies all love their dads and were excited to respond to my inquiries. Each of them has experienced life with a *Dad of the Future*, a dad who has laid the other hats aside for now.

I asked a few simple questions and received back pages of answers because these 12 daughters had a lot to say about their dads. I wanted to know any character traits that would make us the most helpful dads to our grown-up girls. I asked about the role-shifting transition to see if their dads made any deliberate changes in their attitude or actions. I also asked, "Has your dad been there for you during any adult-level problems?" The following pages are gleanings from their answers.

Dad the Sage

By and large, these grown daughters had come to appreciate their dad as a voice of wisdom. For that, I think we can say one role the *Dad of the Future* plays is *Dad the Sage*. Topping the list of wisdom-traits among these ladies' dads, I discovered the following:

- *Listening without judgment*
- *Asking helpful questions without intruding*
- *Guiding without instructing*
- *Calming without devaluing*

Think about each of these for a minute. Some of them are characteristics of any good dad no matter what the age of his girl, but they carry an extra responsibility with them now that she has her own life. The variations between the dad of a young girl and the dad of an older lady are indeed subtle, but these daughters revealed to me the subtle differences make a profound impact. Look for each of the above qualities as you read the glowing comments of these women about their dads, who have now become *Dad the Sage*.

Angela

Dad as an adult parent does really well listening and helping me see the logical solution through my emotional immediate reaction. At work, dealing with my boss or the many men I work with, so many times I will come to Dad emotional (like many females), ranting and raving. He helps me talk it through, and I find that the sensible, logical thing is—most often—really the correct approach to get the best results (instead of my first reaction). He's a "guide in life" when you ask for his advice.

Kimberly

Dad continues to be the spiritual leader he has always been, answering questions I have about my ever-growing relationship with God.

He continues to love me with respect and boundaries. He respects my space so I can grow as an adult at any stage. Always there to guide me and give me advice.

Vernae

As I transitioned into adulthood, my father transitioned into being a helpful guide. I bounce ideas off him without feeling that he is taking over. This is a key in being a parent to an adult child—giving space but being there when I need him, letting me make the decision but giving godly counsel filled with love.

Brecia

As I grew and faced adulthood issues, if I had any problems, Dad was there to be an ear to hear what I had to say. He would only interject when necessary, letting me make the final decision.

But whenever he had something to say, it was based on godly counsel and principles.

Annette

He is ready to discuss faith issues as an adult and how I'm impacted by my faith. He unapologetically will point out when he thinks the Holy Spirit is acting in my life and freely gives advice on how to listen to God more closely.

He is my go-to on career issues and listens patiently and attentively and does not pass judgment.

Years ago, when I was in the final stages of buying my first house, he came to visit and look at it with me. It would have been a huge mistake for me to go through with it because it was a foreclosure in a bad neighborhood with a lot of needed repair. He didn't tell me what to do but guided me through talking about the issues and what I was thinking (at the time I had a bad feeling about the house but didn't think I could back out of the contract).

He asked me probing questions that we discussed until I came to the realization that I really didn't want to buy this house. He made me know that it was ok to back out of the contract even if I lost some money. It turned out to be the best thing I did, backing out of that contract and finding a better home a few years later that I loved and had great experiences with.

Suzanne

Yes—Dad has been there for adult-level problems. Many times. The first thing he does is listen. Always listens. He really never jumps in
without hearing what is happening, what the
worry is, and what I am actually asking him for.
I so appreciate that. In fact, sometimes the listening unravels the issue because as I talk, I hear the
answers and/or begin to understand what I need
to. So that in itself is a gift.

Next, he asks questions—not a lot, but
thoughtful ones. And again, he listens! Last, he
is willing to give advice. And it's usually simple
and sound. Not wordy, not emotion-filled but
logical (I am both emotional *and* wordy, so, oh,
do I need that!) ... but with sympathy.

When I met Randy, Dad was able to step
back and let my husband be the "man in my life"
but still be there when I needed him.

It's really an evolution, I guess, from that
daddy role to mentor/advisor/consultant. I imagine that can be hard—to be the most important
male in the life of a little/teen/young-adult female and then find that "just right" place.

Kathy

Does he help with adult-level problems? YES!
He's been there for all of my problems! I find
that I need his perspective on things when I'm
making a big decision. Our relationship has, of

course, shifted as I grew up. He doesn't yell at me as much anymore! But he still gets exasperated when he thinks I'm failing to value myself enough.

Although he no longer tells me what to do and when to do it, he still points out that decision-making (which has always been an area of weakness for me) needs to come from your gut. My dad makes a decision and moves forward with it. He doesn't contemplate and second-guess all the time. His ability to do that helps me when I'm overwhelmed with all the positives and negatives about my choice. He cuts to the chase and says, 'That sounds like the clear choice; now go make it happen and do it right!' It calms me to hear his conviction that my decision is sound, and, of course, to know he has faith in my ability.

Michelle

He and Mom were such good role models for us with their solid marriage, so I felt confident in all the advice he gave. He was able to be judgment-free and offer advice to help me see all aspects. Even when I went through a divorce, he kept an open mind about the former spouse, sometimes to my chagrin, because I thought he should be all for me … but typical of my dad, he was fair and open to my former husband at times.

As I have grown in adulthood, he has still helped guide me in financial decisions, relationship decisions, and parenting decisions.

These dads must be very proud of their daughters. It is obvious these daughters are proud of their dads. It is not always easy to navigate from being the manager of so many elements of her life to only guiding her and listening to her. These dads decided to let the sails loose instead of tightening them. The irony is that if they had refused to let go of their daughters, they would have had a much smaller positive impact. After these women reached adulthood, none of their fathers ever "told them what to do," yet somehow the girls still gravitated to Dad's advice. Good job, *Dad the Sage*!

Dad the Friend and Equal

When *Dad of the Future* begins to transition into a friendship role, the daddy-daughter relationship becomes more rewarding even for him. Add to that the idea that friends are theoretically equals, and a mutual respect arises. Grown daughters might genuinely enjoy time with that dad as if a good friend has dropped by for coffee.

The dads represented in these lady's memoirs became traveling buddies to their daughters. They shared hobbies and interests. They laughed together. And, as in the case of my wife with her dad, who was a honkytonk entertainer during her youngest years, some got the privilege of dancing with their dad … and not just standing on his toes.

My female friends who helped me with this chapter have all had different experiences with their dads becoming friends to them. For some of them, this equalizing stage was like a chance of redemption for their dad. In other words, maybe he was not very involved in his daughter's life when she was developing, but now that she is older, he can relate better. Whatever the reasons, though, it seems to me that these women truly appreciated the opportunities they have had to learn that their dad is a human being just like them. From what I gather, *Dad the Friend and Equal* allows himself to be vulnerable, a trait that endears him to his new grown daughter-friend.

When my friend Destiny was struggling through her college years, she had a moment with her dad that can go down in history as a great transitional move. I have followed Destiny's dad as a fan for several decades, so this scene impacted me in my hopes to be a great *Dad of the Future*.

I do not know how their entire conversation played out, but I know at one point her dad said, "Tell me what I should have done differently when you were growing up ... And tell me how I can make it up to you now." That moment marked a new day in their relationship from which Destiny's dad would head toward being *Dad the Friend and Equal*.

For more inspiration on getting there yourself one day, read through my other friends' experiences with their wonderful dads. Look for keywords that signify friendship and equality, or mutual respect.

Angela

As an adult, I got to travel with him and share some of his joy of travel and seeing new things. When we were kids, he loved to take us places— and that still holds true, but now on an adult level. Planning a trip together and spending time together has been priceless. [Doing so], we appreciate each other as equals but still feel the father-daughter love.

Having meaningful spiritual conversations, he offers insights and observations and advice but also shares his history and insights as a parent ... but to me as a parent now too.

Kimberly

The first thought to come to mind is respect ... He has always taught respect and given it.

He's the one to always make you smile and laugh when you really didn't want to. He will always be my fun-loving Daddy, making everyone laugh and smile.

Making each other laugh, telling stories, making memories, and taking pictures with each other is a must.

Michelle

Some specific instances are all the times when we had "car talks" where we sat in the dark, in the car, and discussed troubles I was having with a difficult relationship.

I enjoy calling him to talk, and sharing stories and chatting with him, so he has adapted to the girl talk that he didn't use to have time for [Michelle has three sisters who apparently chattered on and on with "girl talk" when they were little].

Stacie

My dad was a better dad as I got older. He became gentler and seemed to understand how fast time was going. He wanted to see me a lot. He told me he was proud of me. He seemed to relate to me better. A teenage girl seemed to scare him.

He talked openly to me as an adult. Didn't seem to "hide" things. Wasn't forced to be the "have it all together" guy. More genuine.

Annette

Dad is great at being objective but somehow always making me feel like he's on my side, even if I've screwed up. When I've had problems with a job, he's been able to share insights from similar experiences of his to validate what I'm feeling and to just let me know that he understands what I'm going through.

Suzanne

I remember worrying in my mid-20s about whether I would EVER meet someone and get married. I talked to my dad a few times about it. One time we stood together at the sink doing dishes after a family dinner. We talked about the meeting-someone thing and my worry about finding the right person and whether they (mom and dad) would like him. Dad said, "Do you really think you would fall in love with someone that we wouldn't like?" That was so reassuring—his trust in me and in my judgment.

One more thing—after I got married and before I had kids, Randy and I went out with my parents and/or hung out at their house late into the night sometimes. That was a precious time to me. We got to be adults with them, couple to couple (even though we were still obviously younger and at a different stage). We got to talk about important and not important stuff and have fun together. I miss that time but hold it close as some of the neatest times with them as an adult.

KaLyndia

The quiet strength of my dad was always behind me. While other family members criticized me for getting "radical for Jesus," he never did.

The times I got to dance with my dad were always special. It was hard to follow his lead on the dance floor because I couldn't keep up with him, but it was always lots of fun to dance with him. It makes me smile just to tell about it.

If these ladies' stories are real, then you and I have a lot to look forward to. Since my girls are all now in their 20s and one is even married, I can say the beginnings of this have been nice. I have always felt like my girls saw me as a friend, but now they are seeing what it is like to have a dad as a friend and an equal. We connect on a level that does not even have to revolve around being father and daughter. We enjoy each other's company, talk about similar interests, laugh at just about everything, and hold each other in high regard. I am looking forward to being *Dad, her Friend and Equal*.

Dad the Grandpa

Here we are, Grandpa, back at the beginning with newborns popping out everywhere. If I drop these little ones, I will feel even worse than if I dropped my own! Will I really have to baby-proof my home again? Please tell me NO!

Thinking about being a grandpa is a little scary to me. For one thing, I just want to be called "Grandpa" or "Granddaddy," but you never know what name that first grandkid is going to pin on you! If I become "PeePee," I will not be writing a grandparenting book in the future. "I'm Their PeePee" is not ok.

Then there is the loss of freedom when your daughter needs a break. I used to leave my girls with my parents all the time and think nothing of it. How was I so inconsiderate? Did I not realize my mom and dad might want to spend Friday night on their own date? Thank you, Mom and Dad, for all the times you watched the Girls for us so we could go have fun.

There are just so many unknowns about becoming Grandpa, I am sure you do not want to rush it. Ready or not, however, grandkids will be here before you know it, so how about a little bit of advice for *Dad of the Future* as he worries about being *Dad the Grandpa* …

Destiny

My dad has been the greatest Pop because he is a champion of my kids. Every time he spends time with them, he brings me a new cute story about them. Besides that, he is not a critic of my parenting. He might let me know if there is something I have to "get ahold of," but he has never criticized my way of getting ahold of it. When it comes to grandparents, sometimes no input is a relief.

Angela

Not only does Dad help me, but he has helped Tara [granddaughter] when she has a prob-lem—discussing her job or frustrations. It actu-ally reminds me of my Grandpa Arnold, who I fondly remember helping talk/listen to me when I was in my teens (and he had come through on a visit as he was driving trucks). I was having friend problems and was unhappy. The warm

Grandpa lap and listening ear, which I think he passed on to our dad, was there for me.

Kathy

As a parent, I can hardly convey adequately how much it means to me to have him as a role model for my children. I feel so sorry for friends that have lost their father before their children really had a chance to know him. I watch him with them, and I am reminded of how lucky I was to grow up with him as my dad. He's always teaching. He can't stop himself. It's embedded in his soul! My kids absolutely revere him, and there is no greater compliment I can give them than to say, "You take after your grandpa!"

Suzanne

Now as a grandpa to my child, he is amazing — always there for Sam and always happy to help me out if I have a scheduling bind and need someone to watch him.

Michelle

One thing many may not know about Dad is that he *loves* babies. Each time I found out I was having a child, it was exciting to know that he would be happy. He has certain ways of handling babies … very carefully holding them so their ears don't fold over or get squished, their hands and feet need to be covered so they don't get cold, and most importantly … don't let their head get misshapen … always turn the head and don't let them lay in one position too long.

When he would first meet the grandchild, it was known he would unwrap that baby to look at each finger and toe and inspect each little detail. His smile and tone of voice when he gets them is so special. He is an awesome grandpa to all ages, as he now has eight grandkids from ages 7 to almost 26!

After sharing about some difficult times she went through in her first marriage and how her dad "acted as 'father' to my three children," Michelle reiterated, "What a great example for his grandchildren."

KaLyndia

My kids loved visiting Granddaddy's because he always cooked a big breakfast and sat with them to watch TV before the other adults woke up. He also let them choose a snack and a soda from his little country store. Kids love that kind of thing. My dad loved my kids.

If that is what it takes, I suppose I do not have to be scared. I know how to love. Bring the grandkids on!

Dad the Rescuer

About two weeks after my daughter was married, she called to see if I might be able to help hang some blinds at her house because she thought she and her husband had broken something. I guess I am *Dad of the Future* after all, being called upon for my grown-up daughter's fix-it problems. And, yes, another hat which *Dad of the Future* wears is *Dad the Rescuer*. Whether that means hanging blinds or loaning money, I think I will like this role. I like helping people, especially if those people are my daughters.

My cousin Andi is one of the women I interviewed about their dads. We only had a moment to speak about him, but Andi's dad definitely fills all the roles of this chapter. He is a really fun grandpa and a genuine friend to his four grown kids. He also has plenty of wisdom as *Dad the Sage*, but what sets Andi's dad aside reveals the heart of this role as *Dad the Rescuer*.

According to Andi, her parents are already the kind who provided a "safety net" below their kids, one that allowed them to take healthy risks in life. But Andi might not have known the full strength of her dad's net until she tragically lost her husband and son within two months of each other. This tragedy left Andi and her two daughters void of the two most important men in their lives. Clay, Andi's husband, could have written this whole book. He was the girl dad of girl dads.

Andi's dad, a man's man, stepped in from day one to do whatever he could do, no matter what the cost to himself. How much a helper he has been cannot be measured, but Andi and her girls have found him everywhere they could have needed him right when they needed him. I do not think he would want to be called *Dad the Rescuer* for what he has done for his daughter and granddaughters, but that is exactly who he has been. His grown-up daughter has faced the greatest trial of her life, and he was there. Sometimes being a rescuer can mean just being there, but some-times it means doing things (whatever things need to be done).

May God help each of us step up to the challenge when our grown-up daughters need *Dad the Rescuer*. Let's look at a couple more snippets from my friends on how their dad was there to help in times of trial.

KaLyndia

My dad supported me financially when I needed it. He helped with down payments on cars, etc. He also slipped me a 20-dollar bill as often as he could just because he knew I could use it. My favorite memories of him helping me, though, were when he would bring me what he loved to call my "stimulus package," a bag of lit-tle things he knew I needed from his little coun-try store.

Kathy

This may be somewhat random but telling you about my dad isn't really hard. He has always been a constant and unwavering source of sup-port. You know when you call someone who is busy and you know they don't have time to talk, but then they hear the littlest quaver in your voice and they say, "Wait, are you OK?" My dad has never failed to make time for me.

He remains my fixer of all things broken. Whenever he comes to visit, I have my Daddy-do list ready to go and he's chomping at the bit to start checking things off. Fixing things for me has always been one of the ways he shows me that he loves me.

Suzanne

When my much-loved dog Milo was dying, my dad's first response was, "Tell me if you want me to be there. I will just sit in the parking lot with you, in the waiting room, or just drive you home. Whatever you need." (My hubby was not in town.)

When my husband's mother died unexpectedly it was the same type of response. When I was struggling with Sam [infant son]—really struggling—he first told me what a good mom I was and then offered to take Sam for a night or, again, whatever might be helpful to me. That is my dad's response, even as a dad to an adult woman. I think his willingness to be there in *whatever role he is needed in* is the thing that is so amazing about him. We grow up, get independent, get partners in life, and have kids, but we still sometimes need our dad.

Suzanne summed that up perfectly. *Dad the Rescuer* is whoever his daughter needs him to be. He will show up wherever she is and do whatever is necessary to help his little girl, his grown daughter.

Dad the Hugger

And as it turns out, almost every woman I have ever talked to about their dad wishes more than anything they could have a hug from him. No matter how many other roles you fill, *Dad of the Future*, it seems you will always have been and always will be *Dad, her First Love*.

Two of the ladies from our panel today have already lost their dads. One of them regretted not being able to contribute more to this chapter, but her dad passed away before he was able to play all the roles of *Dad of the Future*. The other one is my wife, KaLyndia, and she misses her daddy very much.

If either of these ladies had a choice between finding a treasure their dad had left for them or getting to hug him one more time, they would choose the hug. To feel his spirit of kindness and caring, to know that he loves her ... that would be a phenomenal wish granted for either of these women, and that will be where we close our interview with all these grown-up daughters. The things that made them feel hugged by their dads are the most valuable pieces of their memories.

Michelle

I remember as a child I couldn't wait for him to get home from work [so I could] wear his shoes. Now I wait for him to arrive at my house with the anticipation of hugging him and talking and just spending good time together.

Annette

When I really needed him, he has always been there. When I was little, I used to be scared of dying. He comforted me not by sugarcoating anything but being honest with me and pointing me to the Bible, Romans10:9. To this day, that has stuck with me.

Destiny

Dad often reiterates to me, "Grandkids are great, but they are not any greater than any of you were when you were little. You're my first, Baby."

Kathy

We still hug and kiss, and his absolute favorite gift for any holiday is a back rub from me.

Kimberly

Oh! and hugs, hugs are a must. No one can give a hug better than a girl's Daddy, not even a mom.

There You Have It

So there you have it, Dad. Your daughter needs a hug, and she thinks yours are the best in the world. For that, you do not have to be *Dad of the Future*. *Dad Right Now* can run and give her a hug.

If you have come to trust me at all by reading about my journey with my girls, then believe me when I tell you this one last thing: If she had a choice between your hug and a treasure, she would still choose the hug.

And she would love to hear you brag to someone just one more time, "I'm Her Dad!"

Afterword

by KaLyndia Opbroek and The Girls

KaLyndia

Whether you are a new father or a father of a young lady, you need this book! I am convinced my husband Brian is the most qualified person to write about raising girls. When the girls were small, Brian bought a private journal for each one of them. In those journals, he wrote special notes to them about their lives on any given day.

The moments were not always joyful, although most of them were. But in every moment, he wrote with such genuine love, telling them how much he adored them. When the moments were sad, he would gently tell them how much he could relate to their pain and tell them how they could help their own children in the future. When I read back through them, I am so grateful for the man God chose to raise our girls.

In this book, *I'm Her Dad*, you have read about an honest, vulnerable, transparent, giving father who chose to make his journey of raising girls one of the most, if not the most, important adventures of his life. With every daughter, Brian intentionally sought out ways to communicate with them. They adore their father, even in the most intense moments of disagreements.

He was and is their first love. He never lacked the determination to fulfill that role in their lives, and now because he loves them so well, the standard for their husbands is extremely high. Because of their security in his love for them, they have not wavered to settle for less in picking a boyfriend or mate—not to say there have not been some scary moments regarding this topic. However, I have been blown away by Brian's pursuit in filling that spot of their first love. As a mother, I am forever grateful.

As you read each chapter, hopefully you were able to identify with different aspects of his experiences and glean from them or even be challenged to develop your own strategies to help you raise your daughter(s).

KaLeigh

A song by Lee Brice teaches a young man how to love his wife. One of his tips was to "overuse *I love you*." This tip is also key in a father/daughter relationship, and I never lacked this as a child. My dad never went a day without telling me he loves me. I hear other girls describe their dads as "a man of few words." They say, "I know he loves me, but he does not say it often." I believe that one of the main reasons I am the woman I am today—God-fearing, self-sufficient, chaste (and all of the other qualities that I do fiercely aim to be)—is because of this simple thing … my daddy made it a point to tell me I was loved every day.

My daddy's book has offered many tools used in effectively raising girls, but this is one of the most important. Tell your girls you love them. Show them you love them by teaching them to do some of the things outlined in this book. If you do that, you will not have to worry about their safety and decision-making when they are 24 living in a different state, much less a different country like my sister.

Besides all the love my daddy showed me, he also made sure I knew how to change a flat tire, check my own oil, and fix a toilet. You would be surprised how many of my friends have no idea how to do these things. He also taught me to speak my mind and not bottle up my anger. My dad is the smartest person in the world, but he taught me to think for myself.

Bethany

When dad began writing this book, I thought, *This is genius; everyone needs this guide in their life.* Not only does Dad write about the multiple things he and mom did right as parents, but he also is vulnerable enough to mention the wrongs. If anyone is willing to mention where they were at fault, I think it is worth reading about.

As we grew up, Daddy carefully observed each of our personalities and did his best to raise us with *our* perspectives in mind (My mom did too, but this book is not "I'm Her Mom"). My dad intentionally disciplined, instructed, and listened to me. He placed his needs to the side for me (even when I was completely unaware). Most of all, he intentionally pursued me—he was my first love. His example was the reason I could identify a good husband when the time came. My husband is beyond good.

If you desire to be an intentional father, this is your book. I hope you have annotated and highlighted it. Disagree with some of his ideas if you want, but adopt the others as your own.

I had the best daddy. You can be the best dad too.

Callie-Ruth

I cried when my dad called me into his office at the house and said he was writing a book about being our dad. He read me the outline of each chapter and told me what his goal was in writing it and the points he was hoping to drive home. I quietly wept beside him as memories of instances where he proved himself integral in those areas of my life flooded my mind. Then I thought of all my friends who hope to one day have daughters, and I thought of all my friends who are daughters themselves but don't have a daddy who knows how to love them like mine … and I cried some more.

I believe this book has the potential to change the culture of our world. I believe there is brokenness in our societies which can only be healed by the hands of intentional fatherly affection.

If you are wondering how my sisters and I truly feel about our father, you should know that there is no one I admire more or want to spend time with more than him (and our mother). Then again, I have not yet met the man who will eventually take his place, so we will see how long that lasts. LOL

While I cannot adequately speak for my three best friends, the conversations we have had in our adult years prove the similarity of our sentiments. I am the third daughter—the one he calls his redheaded child. My ambition in life is to see the people who come across my path reach their full potentials.

If you are a father of either a boy or a girl—even though this book is specifically geared toward a girl's interaction with her father—this book is just for you. In my 22-plus years on this earth, I cannot begin to count the number of times someone (female or male) has told me they wish my dad were theirs and how many times I have said to myself, *There is no way anyone could be loved more than me.*

This book proves that understanding certain principles is all it takes to make that your reality as a father. Now that you have read it, watch your potential unfold.

Sarah

It is a hard thing to write something that describes my dad. I feel like anything I could ever say of him would never do him justice, and it could never match up to the poetic way he writes about my mom, my sisters, and me.

To tell you how good at parenting my parents are, I have always told them it is unfair to the rest of the world that they have not written a book to tell everyone else how to have strong relationships.

When I was in high school, I took a class under my dad because I wanted to be "forced" to listen to him. All my years growing up, everyone always said he was the best teacher they ever had, and I wanted to experience it myself. My dad can explain things people could otherwise never understand. He can analyze his own weaknesses, turn them into strengths, and show others to do the same. He can make you feel like he is talking straight to you, even if there are thousands of others reading this book.

He can make me feel like the most important person in the world, even though I am one of five for him. My dad is the wisest, smartest, godliest, and most special person in my life (right there with my mommy). I adore him, I look up to him, and I am absolutely in love with him!

Moreover, there is nearly nothing in this world more important for a girl than her relationship with her dad. Yes, dads, the pressure is truly on. But take heart, after reading this book and implementing the tactics written in it, you will undoubtedly have a relationship with your daughter which, for centuries, men have never understood the importance of.

I will say just one more thing about the book you have just read. It could be your "bible" for having an unmatched and phenomenal relationship with your daughter. Thank you for reading it. I am glad you got to meet my dad.

Acknowledgments

As you can see throughout this book, I love my parents. I do not mean to idolize them, but everyone else really missed out by not having them as their parents. Arthur and Marjorie Opbroek made me way back in early March of 1971 up at Malmstrom AFB in Montana. I bet they were snowed in that night. After a nice family dinner and tucking Stephen and Douglas into bed, they must have thought to themselves, *What else should we do tonight?* Then they made me. Good job, Mom and Dad. I am sure it was fun.

I am also grateful to KaLyndia's parents, Yale and Evelyn Poland. Besides raising such a wonderful daughter, they have been a consistent encouragement to us our whole married lives. I could not have asked for more generous, caring, and fun in-laws. I wish Yale were still with us. He was a great dad and a loving granddaddy. We are grateful now for the memories. Our greatest blessing the past few years has been Mom moving closer to us. Now, our evenings are often filled with laughter and purple hull peas.

Next, when it comes to parenting, I would also like to acknowledge our pastors. KaLyndia and I have been at the same church all of our adult lives, so our pastors have been a consistent example to us for over 30 years. First Rodney and Frances Duron, and then Denny and DeAnza Duron, have been perfect examples to us, not just by preaching life-applicable sermons but by living what they have preached.

We love you and are grateful for your investment in our lives.

Considering the whole village that helped raise our girls, I do need to thank the many folks among our family and friends who contributed to their character. Members of SCC, thank you for providing our PKs with a safe environment to grow. To the staff of Evangel Academy—from daycare to graduation—thank you for the sacrifices of working in the world of education and diaper changing. To the Wise & Wonderful group—so many of whom have already passed from this life—thank you for the hours of your investments and kindness while our girls rode in the bus seats next to you and practiced all their singing and storytelling on you. You are the best. We are grateful, also, for the parents of our girls' friends who were such great examples and provided space for our girls to be a part of their lives. And finally, thank you to all the uncles, aunts, and cousins, whom our girls always know they can call when the going gets rough.

As for direct contribution to the production of *I'm Her Dad*, there are a few special people I would like to acknowledge. Mark Donohue (the epitome of a selfless friend), thank you for listening to me so much and for your creative input on the cover design. It turned out perfect. Also, thank you, Darren Shearer and the team at Highbridge, for making this a reality in all its parts.

Next, I need to say a special thank you to the ladies in chapter nine—Andi, Angela, Annette, Brecia, Destiny, June, Kathy, Kimberly, Michelle, Rhonda, Stacie, Suzanne, and Vernae. Thank you for telling us about your dads! Also, I need to say thank you to the handful of guys who came to my little "Dads of Daughters" meetings at the beginning of

2020—Bobby, Chris, Denny-Rodney, Herve, Lake, and Tom. If I had not had to prepare for those meetings, I never would have written this book. Necessity is the mother of getting things done. Thank you.

Of course, *I'm Her Dad* wouldn't mean anything without KaLeigh, Bethany, Callie-Ruth, and Sarah. I love you. Thank you for being who you are. What are the odds that God would put a brunette, blonde, redhead, and raven in the same household and they all come out so perfect? I had my money on you the whole time, and now, because you beat the odds, I got to write a book. Well done, Girls. You had thousands of chances to go in other directions, but you always chose to honor me and Mom. God bless you and keep you. That's what God does for those who honor their parents.

Finally, KaLyndia. KaLyndia is the best wife ever. She's also a phenomenal mom. I'm writing a song about her called "You Should See Their Mom" because that's my response when people tell me how beautiful these girls are. They got more than her beauty, though. Her laugh is contagious. Her faith in God is unwavering. She sacrifices herself for others because that's who she is. She has toughed out some rough times with me and proven to these girls we can live on whatever we find in the pantry. She has spent a lifetime with me telling her, "One day ... One day, KaLyndia, we're going to make it. One day, you'll get to stay with me *richer* instead of *poorer*. One day ... "

KaLyndia, I know you know I know nothing in this book would have happened without you. I tried to say it in the book without taking away from the goal of getting dads to step up and be dads to their daughters, but everyone knows it anyway. Thank you. I love you. :)

Bibliography and Works Consulted

"91 Motivational C.S. Lewis Quotes on Friendship, Heaven & Love." *OverallMotivation*, www.overallmoti-vation.com/quotes/cs-lewis-quotes-friendship-heaven-love/#:~:text=%E2%80%9CFriend-ship%20is%20born%20at%20that%20mo-ment%20when%20one,it%20is%20the%20very%20sign%20of%20His%20presence.%E2%80%9D.

Allman, Tara J. *"An Analysis of the Stereotypes of Preacher's Kids and its Application on their Spouses"* (2007). *Theses, Dissertations, and Capstones*. 13. https://mds.mar-shall.edu/etd/13

Best Buddies, The. https://thebestbuddiesmusic.com/

Bob, et al. "Shakespeare Insults: 50 Shakespearean Insults & Put Downs." *No Sweat Shakespeare*, 10 June 2020. www.nosweatshakespeare.com/resources/shakespeare-insults/.

Bostrom, Meg. Framework Institute, 2001, pp. 1–38. *The 21st Century Teen: Public Perception and Teen Reality*.

Cunningham, Loren, et al. *Why Not Women?: A Fresh Look at Scripture on Women in Missions, Ministry, and Leadership*. YWAM Publishing, 2014.

Eğeci, İ.S., Gençöz, T. Factors Associated with Relationship Satisfaction: Importance of Communication

Skills. *Contemp Fam Ther* 28, (2006): 383–391. https://doi.org/10.1007/s10591-006-9010-2

Fay, Jim. *Helicopters, Drill Sergeants, and Consultants: Parenting Styles and the Messages They Send.* Love and Logic Press, 1994.

Gladwell, Malcolm. *Outliers: Why Some People Succeed and Some Don't.* Little Brown & Co., 2008.

Lansky, Vicki. *Baby Proofing Basics: How to Keep Your Child Safe.* Book Peddlers, 2002.

Lynch, James J. *The Broken Heart: The Medical Consequences of Loneliness.* Basic Books, 1979.

Manhart, Lisa E., and Laura A. Koutsky. "Do Condoms Prevent Genital HPV Infection, External Genital Warts, or Cervical Neoplasia?" *Sexually Transmitted Diseases,* vol. 29, no. 11, (2002): 725–735. doi:10.1097/00007435-200211000-00018.

McManners, Hugh. *The Complete Wilderness Training Manual.* Metro Books, an Imprint of Sterling Publishing Co., Inc., 2015.

Meyer, John C. "Humor as a Double-Edged Sword: Four Functions of Humor in Communication." *Communication Theory,* vol. 10, no. 3, (2000): 310–331. doi:10.1111/j.1468-2885.2000.tb00194.x.

Pittman, Marc, and Mark Wangrin. *Raising Cole: Developing Life's Greatest Relationship, Embracing Life's Greatest Tragedy: A Father's Story.* Health Communications, 2004.

"Sex Offender Registry/Search." *RecordsFinder,* 26 April 2020. recordsfinder.com/sex-offenders/.

Stewart, John Robert., et al. *Together: Communicating Interpersonally*. Roxbury Publ. Co., 2004.

Taken (2008)

Welborn, Vickie. "Show Features Justin Bloxom Murder." *Shreveporttimes.com*, 30 Mar. 2015. www.shreveport-times.com/story/news/local/2015/03/30/justin-bloxom-investigation-discovery-amy-fletcher-brian-horn-murder-desoto-parish-dustin-rosegrant-adam-ewing-keith-banta/70695842/.

Wolak, Janis, et al. "Online 'Predators' and Their Victims: Myths, Realities, and Implications for Prevention and Treatment." *American Psychologist*, vol. 63, no. 2, (2008): 111–128. doi:10.1037/0003-066x.63.2.111.

Wolgemuth, Robert D. *She Calls Me Daddy: 7 Things You Need to Know about Building a Complete Daughter*. Tyndale House Publishers, Inc., 2014.

"Victoria Secunda Quotes (Author of When You and Your Mother Can't Be Friends)." Goodreads, www.goodreads.com/author/quotes/48987.Victoria_Secunda.

Index

10,000
  hours, 4
  times, 1
24-Hour Rule, The, **158**
4th of July, 196
7 Habits of Highly Effective Teens, The, 153
99 Theses, 197
absence, father, 79
abuse, 37, 72, 84, 85, 127
acts of kindness, 92, 93
ADD, 186
ADHD, 186
Adolescent Psychology, 2
advertising, 178
Affection, Her Heart's Gateway, 79
Alcohol and Drugs, 175
allowance, 134, 136, 184
Allowance Log, 136
Alzheimer's, 218
Amber, 29, 30
Amends, Having to Make, 130
America, 26, 82, 156, 158, 162, 187, 196

American Psychology, 31
Amish, 142
Amoruso, Sophia, 153
Andi, 235, 248
Angela, 221, 228, 232, 248
anger, 4, 37, 40, 77, 127, 213
Annette, 223, 229, 248
anorexia nervosa, 79
apologies, 55
Apologies, Making, **69**
approval, 100, 217
arguments, 66, 68, 69, 99
  delivering, 55, **66**, 68
assailant, 29
ASVAB, 162
atheist, 201
attention span, 132
Attentions, Loving, **87**
attractions, 177, 208
auditory processing disorder, 186
Australia, 162
Autism, 186
autograph book, 217
avalanche, 21

Baby Proofing/Child Proofing, 15, 17, 42, 231, 252

Bach, 99

bad guy, 25, 26, 110, 111

baker's dream, 156

bar mitzvah, 141, 142

barbed wire, 22

bat mitzvah, 142

Beethoven, 99

believer, 201, 214

belittling, 114

Best Buddies, The, 99, 251

Bethany, viii, 83, 169, 218, 243, 249

Bible, 118, 156, 206, 213, 215, 239

bitterness, 208, 219

blonde, 249

Bloxom, Amy, 29, 253

Bloxom, Justin, 29

bluff, 107, 108, 133, 134, 192

Bob's Burgers, 89

boundaries, 11, 16, 26, 45, 47, 206, 222

boys, xi, 17, 23, 24, 25, 26, 30, 41, 82, 110, 156, 193

Brecia, 222, 248

Brice, Lee, 242

Brooklyn Nine Nine, 89

brother(-s), 28, 73, 107, 195, 213

brunette, 249

Bryan Wells, 27, 36

Buddy, 129

cab, 29, 30

Callie Ruth, viii, 83, 89, 162, 244, 249

car privileges, 134, 135

cardiovascular system, 54

cervical cancer, 35

Charlie's Angel, viii

chat rooms, 30, 31, 35, 177

chauvinist, 26, 92

Checks and Balances, 213

Chivalry, as a loving attention, 91

Christmas, 17, 95

Clay, 235

coincidence, 56, 162

comics' basic no-no's, 63

Communications Director, Dad, 51

compass, 6, 77

compassion, 179, 201

compliments, 98, 99

compound interest, 184

concealed weapons management, 28

condoms, 35, 49, 252

confidentiality, 70, 71, 72, 73, 193

conscience, 25, 112, 124,
128, 131, 145, 146, 148,
159, 172, 193, 210
Consumer Report, 19
Conversation, Carrying a,
73
corporal punishment,
127, 129
counseling, 72, 114, 132,
154, 185
country store, 234, 236
Covey, Sean, 153
COVID-19, 82, 162
credit score, 184
criticism, 39, 40, 93
Cultural Norms, 182
cultural quilt, 182
Cunningham, Loren, 170,
251
cup-bearer's dream, 156
Curie, Marie, 144
Daddy Let Me Drive, 164
Daddy's Hands, 128
Daddy-do list, 237
Dalai Lama, the, 204
dance/dancing, viii, 44,
88, 103, 226, 230
danger, physical, 17, 19,
37
dating, 24
de Becker, Gavin, 147

Dead Man's Talk, 193,
194
Dean of Discipline, Dad
the, 107
Death and Dying, 178,
179, 180, 198
Deborah, 143
decision-making skills,
150, 154
demon, 118
Destiny, 160, 227, 232
devaluing, 221
discernment, 139, 147
disciples, 6, 7
disclosure, 74
divine, 199, 202
call, 144
characteristics of love,
77
connection, 146
moments, 203
voice, 146
divorce, 102, 183, 225
DNA, 17, 149
Do Hard Things: A Teenage
Rebellion Against Low
Expectations, 153
doctor, 64, 192
at baby birth, 203
in the ER, 202
dogmatic, 210
donkey, 206

Donohue, Mark, 248
Do-over, 59, 60
doozy, 169
Down by the Creek Bank, 168
Dr. Phil, 175
drainage, emotional, 37, 40, 41
dream actualization, 154
dreams, night time, 155, 160
drill sergeant, 107, 200, 252
Duke, 160
Duron, DeAnza, 99, 247
Duron, Denny Sr., 247
Duron, Rodney and Frances, 247
Dweck, Carol S., 153
dysgraphia, 186
dyslexia, 186
Earhart, Amelia, 143
Eastwood, Clint, 110
Edison, 4
Education and Academics, 185
ego, 124
electronic device, 29, 30
emergency(-ies), 17, 19, 20, 21, 42, 44, 62, 122
emotions, 35, 39, 46, 86, 127, 177, 219

empathy, 126, 174, 199
endpoint, in storytelling, 63
Enneagram, 109, 166
equality, 92, 143, 227
Eskimo kisses, 83
evolution of thought, 191
Ewing, Dr. Col. Bruce, 129
exit
    from a conversation, 55, 74
    from a potentially dangerous situation, 20
expectations, lack of clarity in, 119
experimentation, 23, 35, 190
external motivators, 138
Facebook, 64, 82, 97
failure, 4, 6, 9, 119
    converted, 3
    fear of, 16
Fasting and Prayer, **161**, 162, 163
FBI, 163
fear, 18, 22, 73, 116, 158, 192
    healthy, 28, 107
    of failure, 16
    of rejection, 16

of the unknown, 16
Fear, The Gift of, 147
feedback, 58
feminism, 92
fight-or-flight, 108
file-sharing programs, 32
finish line, 80, 219
five love languages, 91
flirtations, 32
Flow of Concern, 146, 147
forgiveness, 55, 59, 118,
    131, 194, 195, 220
Form 1040, 171
free market, 184
Fresh Eyes, 160, 161
Friend and Equal, Dad
    the, 226, 227, 231
friendship, 72, 125, 173,
    200, 251
Frustrating Errors, 111,
    112, 205
Future, Dad of the, *217*
Gandhi, 204
gap year, 187
generational transfer, 149
genius, 53, 243
Girl Boss, 153
giving her away, 218, 219
Goal-orientation, 153
gossip, 59, 71
GPS, 44
grace, 130, 131

Grace, 204
Graham, Billy, 204
Grandpa Arnold, 232
Grandpa, Dad the, 231
Greenwood, Lee, 195
grounded, 130, 136, 138
Guard Your Heart, 42
gun safety, 19
Guru, Dad the, *201*
Hallmark cards, 98
Harris, Alex and Bret, 153
Hats, Dad's, *1*
helicopter parenting, 172
help-mate, 143
Her First Love, Dad, *77*
hidden treasure, 16
Holy Family, 141
honesty, 8, 72, 110, 126,
    173, 174, 199
honkytonk, 226
hooks, 74
horn, 18
HPV, 35, 49, 252
humility, 62, 174, 199
Humor, **62**, 63, 99, 174,
    199, 252
    standards of, 63
hunger, spiritual, 211
hypocrisy, 112
I love you vs. Love you,
    93

ignorance, 17, 21, 22, 35, 42
image of God, 143, 144
impasse, 197
injustice, 213
insecurity, 8, 147
Instagram, 31, 66, 97, 147
insurance, 21, 131, 184
interpersonal communication, 53, 54, 70
interruptions, 60, 61, 62, 68
interview, job, 54
Introductions, Initiating, 61
intruding, 221
Intuition, 154
Issues Management Handbook (IMHB), 189
Issues Manager, Dad the, *171*
Jackson, Alan, 164
Jesus, 6, 7, 45, 48, 80, 89, 141, 142, 145, 206, 211, 230
Joan of Arc, 146
Job, the parent, 208
John the Baptist, 80
Joseph and Mary, 45
journal, x, 7, 75, 96, 241
judgment

better..., 124
not passing..., 223
skewed..., 189
trusting her..., 230
KaLeigh, viii, 83, 242, 249
KaLyndia, 3, 24, 203, 230, 234, 236, 238, 247, 249
Karate, 29
Kathy, 224, 233, 248
Keith, Toby, 195
Kimberly, 222, 228, 248
kissing, 24, 120
knee jerking, 192
Kung Fu, 28
Language of the Heart, 54
Lansky, Vicki, 15, 252
last word, the, 68, 69
leadership, 144, 164, 165, 166, 169
learning challenges, 186
learning styles, 186
Lecturing, 38, 132
Letter vs. Spirit, 204
Leverage, 133, 135
Lewis, C.S., 173
Liberator, Dad the, 141
lifejacket, 22
Lifestyle of Love, 101
lock-down drills, 20
Louisiana, 17, 19
Love Never Fails, ix
Lowery, Fred, 104

Lynch, James J., 54, 76,
252
magnetism, 177
Malmstrom AFB, 247
manipulation, 183, 197
marijuana, 175
Mary and Joseph, 45
Mary, the disciple and
friend of Jesus, 211
mate, 103, 143, 242
mechanical malfunctions,
22
melting pot, 182
memory, 5, 23, 58, 75, 95,
96, 113, 117, 123, 173,
174, 199
mentors, 160
messaging, 31, 64, 65, 97
Michelle, 225, 228, 229,
233, 234, 248
Milo, 237
*Mindset: The New
Psychology of Success*,
153
Money
and Gifts, as loving
attentions, 89
as an issue to manage,
183
Montana, 247
morals, 27, 178, 205
Mother Theresa, 143

Motivation Check, The,
123
multiple sclerosis, 202
Muslim, 142
mutual respect, 226, 227
Myers-Briggs, 109
naivety, 21, 172
narcissist, 66, 98
National Anthem, 195
National Guard, 162
navigator's trio, 6
Neeson, Liam, 27
nervous system, 154
Netflix, 88, 153
nincompoop, 25
non-believer, 201
Olson, Jeff, 153
One Direction, 156
Opbroek, Arthur (the
author's dad), x, 73,
102, 107, 169, 213, 247
Opbroek, Douglas (the
author's brother), 28,
195, 213, 247
Opbroek, Marjorie (the
author's mom), x, 73,
95, 102, 231, 247
Opbroek, Stephen (the
author's brother), 73,
247
open drink, 27

opinions and feelings,
190, 191, 192
optical illusion, 182
Orman, Suze, 184
Outbursts, Violent, 113
oversight, 149
paradox, 43, 68, 196
parents
  Jesus', 45, 141
  the author's, x, 5, 6, 7,
    24, 134, 247
  the author's wife's, 247
Parks and Rec, 88
Passive Aggression, 121,
  123
patriotism, 163, 195
Paul the Apostle, 4
pause button, 38
Pause-it, 60
PDA--Public Display of
  Affection, 82, 97
Pearl of Great Price, 16
PeePee, 231
peer pressure, 176
penny per page, 137
pepper spray, 28
personal information, 31,
  32
personality type, 109
PG
  journal, x
  rating, 174, 175

Phillip, 215
phone access, 134, 135
Pittman, Marc, 193
PK--Preacher's Kid, 8, 9,
  73
Pledge of Allegiance, 196
plot, in storytelling:, 63
poem, 93, 98, 217
poker face, 192
Poland, Evelyn, 247
Poland, Yale, 234, 247
Politics and Religion, 180,
  181
Pollyanna, 118
poorer, 249
Pop, 232
Pope, the, 204
pornography, 33
posting, 31, 32, 64, 65, 66,
  98
predators, 17, 22, 27, 29,
  30, 31, 32, 33, 36, 37, 65,
  177
prejudices, 183
Prep-talk Pep-talks, **57**
president, viii, x, 53, 164
pride, vii, 22, 73, 77, 123,
  124
Priorities List, 152, 153
private messaging, 31
Project Manager, Make
  Her a..., **167**

prophet, 57
prophetic worship, 212
Pros and Cons, 150, 159,
  162
public shaming, 116, 117
punishment, 125, 126,
  129, 134
  that fits the crime, 129
purple hull peas, 247
Quinceañera, 142
Raising Cole, 193
RAM, 154, 155
Ramadan, 142
Ramsey, Dave, 184
Randy, 224, 230
ratings, 175
raven, 249
real, being, 35, 172, 173,
  178, 189
Reciprocal Consequences,
  129, 130
red flags, 214
redhead(-ed), 18, 245, 249
refrigerator, 46
relationship satisfaction,
  54, 76, 251
Religious Rebukes, 117
Rescuer, Dad the, 234,
  235, 236, 237
rest in peace, 12
reverse psychology, 61
richer, 249

Rites of Passage, 141
rod, 127, 129, 131, 132,
  133, 137, 138
role-shift, 220
Romans10
  9, 239
Rumspringa, 142
Rutherford, Irvin, 26
Safe Haven, 46, 47
safety net, 235
Sage, Dad the, 221, 226,
  235
sails, 81, 226
Sam, 233, 237
Sarah, viii, 83, 123, 163,
  245, 249
sarcasm, 114, 115, 116
Scott, Steven K., 153
seatbelt, 153
Secunda, Victoria, 79, 80,
  104, 253
Security Detail, Dad, 15
self-help, 93, 153
self-image, 85, 99
self-motivation, 154
setting, in storytelling, 63
sex offender, 26, 35, 252
sex trafficking, 27
sexuality, 176, 178, 198
Shakespeare(-an), 116,
  251

She Calls Me Daddy, x, xi,
5, 10, 30, 48, 61, 76, 253
Sher, Coach, 158
shoebox, 95, 96
Sifu, 28
*Simple Steps to Impossible
Dreams*, 153
sleepovers, 43
Slight Edge, The, 153
smell
marijuana, 175
the rankest compound
of villanous..., 116
Smith, Jaclyn, viii
snobbery, 61
social anxiety, 34
social class, 185
social media, 31, 64, 65,
66, 97, 98, 116, 188
softball, 57, 158, 161
space-stare, 52
Spanking, 128
Specialized Knowledge,
Seek her…, 166
Spirit vs. Letter, 204
spirituality, 210
spousal love, 102
Stacie, 229
stalker, 148
STD, 35
Stephen-King, 118
Sticky Boobs, 12

stocking, 95
Storytelling, 62
style, sense of, 165
Sugar and Spice, vii
Sunday School, 43, 211,
212
survival guide/training
manual, 17
survival-of-the-fittest, 108
Suzanne, 224, 230, 233,
237, 248
Swanson, Ron, 89
taboo, 46, 117, 176
Taken (2008), 27, 253
Tara, 232
Tattletales, 71
tea parties, viii
Teaching Moments, 56
texting, 44, 64, 65, 66, 70
Thanksgiving, 169
thoughts
maybe God's answer to
your prayer, 207, 209
motivated by love, 77
sexual, 35, 177
Time, as a loving
attention, 87
toe-dancing, viii
Tom, 37
touch
loving, 81, 82, 83, 84
the trouble with, 84

the trouble with no, 85
Tourette's Syndrome, 186
tractor, 213
trauma, 17
treasure hunt, 156, 157
Trial & Error, **109**, 110,
 127
trustworthiness, 71, 72,
 73, 119
ugliness, 40, 67
Uncle Sam, 3, 163
University of New
 Hampshire, 31, 33
Vernae, 222, 248
vetting, 211, 212, 213
victimization, 31, 35
virtues, 110
voices, 28, 113, 145
Voices, the song, 145
vulnerable(-ity)
 in a good way, 11, 77,
  227, 241, 243
 to predators, 30, 31, 32,
  34, 35, 42, 177
Web of Lies, 30
weddings, 219
weekend freedom, 134,
 135
Whataburger, 44
wildlife, 22
win-win, 25, 133, 135

Wolgemuth, Robert, x, xi,
 5, 30, 31, 48, 61, 253
words, careful, 93
Worry less… watch
 more, 32
written notes, 95, 96
WWJD, 145
X-rated, 33
yelling, 41, 68, 112, 113
You Should See Their
 Mom, 249
Young, Chris, 145
youth group, 134, 169,
 212
YouTube, 147, 167, 199